Financial Accounting

Financial Accounting
A Practical Introduction

Ilias G. Basioudis

Financial Times
Prentice Hall
is an imprint of

Harlow, England • London • New York • Boston • San Francisco • Toronto
Sydney • Tokyo • Singapore • Hong Kong • Seoul • Taipei • New Delhi
Cape Town • Madrid • Mexico City • Amsterdam • Munich • Paris • Milan

Pearson Education Limited
Edinburgh Gate
Harlow
Essex CM20 2JE
England

and Associated Companies throughout the world

Visit us on the World Wide Web at:
www.pearsoned.co.uk

First published 2010

© Pearson Education Limited 2010

ISBN: 978-0-273-71429-3

British Library Cataloguing in Publication Data
A catalogue record for this book is available from the British Library

Library of Congress Cataloging-in-Publication Data
Basioudis, Ilias G. (Ilias Grigorios)
 Financial accounting : a practical introduction / Ilias Basioudis. — 1st ed.
  p. cm.
 Includes bibliographical references and index.
 ISBN 978-0-273-71429-3 (pbk.)
1. Accounting. I. Title.
 HF5628.B37 2009
 657—dc22

                                          2009043576

10 9 8 7 6 5 4 3 2 1
14 13 12 11 10

Typeset in 10.5/13pt Sabon by 35
Printed in Great Britain by Henry Ling Ltd., at the Dorset Press, Dorchester, Dorset

The publisher's policy is to use paper manufactured from sustainable forests.

Contents

Preface

This book primarily intends to address a specific gap in the current market, namely the shortage of a comprehensive number of examples and numerical exercises together with fully worked answers in financial accounting. In addition, each chapter provides brief guidance and serves as a reminder of the key points in each topic area of financial accounting.

The book is designed mainly as a supplementary workbook to any key introductory textbook in financial accounting taken by students studying for a degree in accounting or business. In general, the book is useful to students taking a degree course in accounting or other business studies degree at undergraduate university level. It will also be attractive to students reading towards a relevant professional qualification offered by the professional accountancy bodies and associations. The book could also be used at the postgraduate level where the detailed mechanics of financial statement preparation are taught. It is also offered as a useful revision tool.

Learning financial accounting is like learning a different language and, as such, lots of practice is required. Apparently, financial accounting is not a particularly popular subject among first-year students. Students usually find the first-year introductory financial accounting module quite challenging and demanding. I regularly remind students to do as much practice as they can at the introductory level of financial accounting, and I consistently hear students asking me to provide them with extra numerical questions and exercises. Hence, the book you hold in your hands, *Financial Accounting: A Practical Introduction*, will hopefully fulfil the students' needs for more practice, and equip them with an essential study aid when studying financial accounting or revising for exams. Attempting a large number of accounting questions provides students with the necessary self-assurance and familiarity required to deal with the more difficult aspects of financial accounting.

Each chapter begins with brief notes which are designed to refresh your memory and understanding of the subject area. The notes in each chapter are *not* a substitute for a textbook; rather they are a *reminder* of the key points in each topic area and provide brief *guidance* on particularly knotty points or areas which can cause problems to students. So, imagine this book as a miniature skeleton or concise version of the standard traditional textbook in financial accounting. The core material is covered by the standard textbook and, therefore, you will not find excessively lengthy explanations, case studies or unnecessary illustrations in the notes of this book. Each chapter focuses on specific learning outcomes that students will need to know factual content for. It is important to make it clear that this book complements the traditional textbook and should be bought in addition to, not instead of, it.

Financial Accounting: A Practical Introduction benefits students in many ways:

- it encourages them to learn and fulfil the learning objectives of the subject;
- it aids them in obtaining the necessary confidence to tackle financial accounting issues and advanced exercises;
- it demonstrates how to solve the numerical exercises using the suggested answers;
- it assists learners to convince themselves that they have understood the subject material;
- it facilitates students to take control of their own learning; and
- it supports them towards their revision requirements.

Educators will also find this book valuable for a number of reasons:

- they may use it to introduce new accounting topics at overview level before delving into the detail typically included in a standard-size textbook;
- teachers may use it as an efficient means to re-visit accounting topics towards the end of an accounting course; and
- they may ask students to attempt a specific number of questions from this book at the end of each lecture/session.

Finally, this book will also benefit both educators and students of advanced financial accounting modules who require an efficient means of revising the fundamental aspects of the subject matter.

The current edition of the book has only included the *basics* in financial accounting. Like any subject, the basics are the most important. The students must understand *what* they are doing, *why* they are doing it, and *how* they should go about doing it. The second edition of the book may include some exam questions from professional bodies; these are currently on the website (www.pearsoned.co.uk/basioudis) and only available to lecturers who adopt the book. If you have any other suggestions and comments, you can contact the publishers in the first instance.

If you are looking for the fun and challenge of self-practicing, self-testing or preparing for a financial accounting examination, then this book is designed to help you. You can check your own standard, monitor your progress, and learn things that you hadn't picked up from your main textbook. Assessing and revising systematically the knowledge gained in the subject matter is an important and critical step in your understanding of financial accounting, and this book will assist you in accomplishing this. Most importantly, this book can be used to explicitly guide you in your study and assist you in judging your strengths and weaknesses.

One final point: before you start reading or attempting to tackle any questions from this book, I would like you to arm yourself with a thick pad of blank paper, a pen and possibly a calculator, because this is a practical subject, and I want you to 'doodle' as little as possible and be engaged in the subject matter as much as possible. Remember, novels are meant to be read in bed or in front of the TV or computer screen, but not this kind of book! In addition, I would encourage you to pass the temptation of looking at the answer first and then start 'solving' an exercise, but rather try to work through each chapter notes and then concentrate on how best you can answer each question. If you turn directly to the solutions without doing the necessary self-practice, then the value of the book will be lessened, and you will not be able to spot your weaknesses. Further, you must work slowly through as many of the questions in this book as possible, and do not resort to the answer the moment you get stuck. Attempt to get 'unstuck' by yourself, and you will find this attempt to be a very valuable exercise in developing your ability to think clearly and logically.

A note to students and lecturers: all companies across the European Union (EU), including the UK, that are listed on an EU stock exchange, are obliged today to follow the international accounting standards in the preparation of their final accounts. All other companies and business organisations in the UK continue to use the 'old' UK accounting standards. This book has *not* adopted the 'new' terminology and rules applied by the international accounting standards. Nonetheless, you can find below a very simple comparative table that provides a quick view of the key terminology changes between the UK and international standards.

Traditional UK accounting standards terminology	*International accounting standards terminology*
Profit and loss account	Income statement
Sales/turnover	Revenue
Provision for doubtful debts	Allowance for doubtful debts (or Allowance for trade receivables)
Profit and loss account (on balance sheet)	Retained earnings
Exceptional item	No equivalent
Extraordinary item	No equivalent
Balance sheet	Balance sheet (also, Statement of financial position)
Fixed assets	Non-current assets
Trade debtors	Trade (or Accounts) receivable
Stock	Inventory
Current liabilities (or Creditors: amounts falling due within one year)	Current liabilities
Trade creditors	Trade (or Accounts) payable
Long-term liabilities (or Creditors: amounts falling due after more than one year)	Non-current liabilities
Long-term loan/debenture	Loan note

The author is grateful to the following bodies for permission to reproduce copies of their past examination questions: the Association of Chartered Certified Accountants (ACCA), the Institute of Chartered Accountants in England and Wales (ICAEW), the Institute of Certified Bookkeepers, the London Chamber of Commerce and Industry, the Chartered Institute of Management Accountants (CIMA) and the Institute of Certified Management Accountants (ICMA). The set of examination questions from the professional bodies is currently only available to lectures who adopt the book in their module. The answers to questions on the website are my own and have not been supplied by any of the examining bodies.

I would like to sincerely thank my wife, Iliana Anagnou-Basioudis, for her tolerance and understanding during the period of writing this book, and Ms Basia Nowakowska for her immaculate secretarial assistance. Also, the team from Pearson, Dawn Booth, copy-editor, Tim Parker, senior desk editor, and Matthew Smith, editorial director, for the wonderful cooperation we have had over the past few months.

Finally, this book was being written in a period when two very important events took place in my life: the birth of my first son, Philippos Grigorios Callum, and the sad and unexpected passing of my mother. This book is dedicated to both of them.

Ilias G. Basioudis
Summer 2009

Chapter 1

Financial statements and the accounting equation

This chapter briefly covers the following topics:

- Introduction to financial statements
- The accounting equation
- More about financial statements

Introduction to financial statements

The financial statements are the end product of the accounting process, they portray the company in financial terms, and they relate to specific date or cover a specific period of business activity.

WHAT do *YOU* want to know about a business at the end of a period?

1 How well has the business performed *during* the period.

→ Then you look at the Profit and Loss Account (P&L a/c), (based on the international accounting standards, it is also known as the income statement).

2 What is the business's financial position *at the end* of the period.

→ Then you look at the balance sheet.

3 How much cash has the business generated and spent *during* the period.

→ Then you look at the cash flow statement.

The accounting equation

In accounting, there is an important relationship between assets, liabilities and owners' equity. This relationship is captured by the following equation, which basically states that for any business and at any time:

Assets – Liabilities = Owners' equity

Equally,

Owners' equity + Liabilities = Assets

The above equation is called the **accounting equation**. The total assets of the business minus the debts (liabilities) of the business (the result of which is referred to as the *net assets*) equals the owners' equity.

The owners' equity is the amount the owners have invested in the business, plus any additional earnings (net profit) of the business. In the same way, the owners' equity is the amount of money that the business owes back to the owners and, as a result, it can be seen as another form of debt the business is obliged to pay.

Therefore, based on the second equation above, the total assets of a business are financed through creditors (liabilities), also known as the 'outsider' claims, and/or owners (owners' equity), also known as the 'insider' claims.

Changes in the owners' equity

Profits (P) are an addition to a business's opening capital (OC), while losses (L) are a reduction to a business's opening capital. Opening capital may also be increased by a new injection of funds – new capital (NC) – introduced by the owners. Opening capital is reduced by drawings (D), being withdrawals of funds made by the owners. Therefore, the increase in the owner's equity (OE) of a business – also, known as the closing capital – over a period depends on these three factors, and can be calculated by the following equation:

$$OE = OC + P \text{ (or } - L) + NC - D$$

It is usual to re-arrange the above relationship to provide a formula for calculating the profit (P) or the loss (L) made by a business during a period.

More about the financial statements

Profit and loss account

The profit and loss account (or income statement) is a financial statement which illustrates the financial effects of a profit or loss of all operating and trading activities of a business during a specified period of time (normally a 12-month period).

Based on the matching principle, a profit and loss account matches the revenue earned in a period with the costs (expenses) incurred in earning it in the same period. It is usual to distinguish between a gross profit (sales revenue less the cost of goods sold) and a net profit (being the gross profit less the expenses of selling, distribution, administration, etc.).

Revenue is defined as income of the business which is earned through the sale of goods (stock), or the performance of services. For example, the fees an accountant earns for providing accounting services to her clients is her revenue. It increases the profits of a business and, hence, the value of owners' equity (and, in effect, decreases the value of liabilities and increases the value of assets).

Expenses are costs incurred in the normal course of business as a result of the revenue earning process. For example, salaries, rent, advertising, telephone expenses, internet, electricity, etc. They reduce the profits of a business and, hence, the value of owners' equity (and, in effect, increase the value of liabilities, and decrease the value of assets).

At the end of each accounting period, profit (or loss) determination occurs in two stages: *first*, a *gross profit or loss* arising from the sale of goods (minus the cost of goods sold) is calculated. *Second*, other expenses for the period are subtracted from the gross profit for the period. The difference between gross profit and other expenses, where gross profit exceeds expenses, is the *net profit* (or the net income). Where expenses exceed the gross profit, the difference is the *net loss* for the period.

Profit/loss is the net amount earned by income-producing activities (after taking away the expenses) and kept for use in the business.

Balance sheet

A balance sheet is a detailed listing of the assets, liabilities and owners' equity of a business at a given moment. It is designed to illustrate the financial position of the business at a given point in time.

The balance sheet is based on the accounting equation and includes three broad headings: assets, liabilities and owner's equity.

Assets are defined as the economic (or physical) resources which are controlled by the business and are expected to produce a benefit in the future. In other words, these resources are expected to contribute to the future revenue earning capability of the business.

Assets are split into: (1) fixed (or non-current) assets; and (2) current assets.

1 *Fixed assets* are assets held by a business over more than 12 months. They are depreciated over their useful lives so as to spread their cost over the accounting periods which benefit from their use. Examples of fixed assets include: property, plant, equipment, fixtures and fittings, motor vehicles, building, land, patents, trademarks, franchises, copyrights and goodwill.

2 *Current assets* are cash and other short-lived assets which will soon (normally within a year) be converted into cash in the course of the business's normal operations. Examples of current assets include: stock (or inventory), trade debtors (or receivables), bank, cash and prepaid expenses.

Liabilities are the 'outsider' claims or economic obligations that have to be paid off to outsiders in the future. They are split into: (1) current liabilities; and (2) long-term (or non-current) liabilities.

1 *Current liabilities* are claims that need to be paid off within 12 months. Examples of current liabilities include: trade creditors (or payables), accrued expenses, short-term loan and bank overdraft.

2 *Long-term liabilities* are claims that are due after more than 12 months. Examples of long-term liabilities include: long-term loan, debentures and mortgages.

Owners' equity, as seen above, represents the '*insider* claims' of a business, and is matched in the balance sheet by assets and liabilities. The owners' equity includes the opening capital, the profit or loss, new capital introduced by owners and withdrawals made by the owners (see also above the subsection 'Changes in the owners' equity').

Cash flow statement

The cash flow statement lists cash payments and receipts for the period, and shows the mechanisms within a business that generate and absorb cash. It provides information as to the liquidity and solvency position of a business.

The statement is accompanied by a number of reconciliations and a series of notes which disclose the movements of stocks, debtors and creditors as part of a business's normal operations. It is published in a prescribed format.

The profit and loss account and the balance sheet do not provide any information about the source and disposition of the cash (apart from the opening and closing cash and bank balances in the balance sheet).

Short questions

Question
Ilias starts a business and introduces capital of £10,000. He also obtains a loan of £6,000 to purchase fixed assets. What is the amount of his opening net assets?

Answer
The accounting equation states that:

Equity = Assets − Liabilities (= Net assets)

So Ilias's equity (capital) is £10,000 and his net assets are therefore also £10,000. Similarly, total assets are £16,000, and total liabilities are £6,000, so the net assets are only £10,000.

Question
A company has the following assets and liabilities at 31 December: premises £30,000; trade creditors £4,000; stock £9,000; amounts owed for rent at 31 December £900; cash in hand £2,500; balance at bank overdrawn £3,400;

trade debtors £3,600; equipment £5,000. a) How much is the company worth – i.e. what is its capital (equity) on 31 December? b) If, six months later, the capital has increased by £4,000, what reasons could account for this? c) If, six months later, the capital has decreased by £2,000 what could be the reasons for this decrease?

Answer

a By using the accounting equation [Equity = Assets – Liabilities], we get: £41,800.

b Profits or introduction of new capital.

c Losses or drawings of capital by owner(s).

Question

The owner of a business introduced new capital of £8,000 during the year and withdrew £2,500 cash for his private use. The profit earned by a business in 2008 was £68,500. If the net assets at the beginning of 2008 were £100,000, what were the closing net assets?

Answer

The 'changes in owners' equity' equation states that:

$$OE = OC + P + NC - D$$

Opening capital (OC) equals the net assets at the beginning of 2008, which is £100,000. So,

$$OE = £100,000 + 68,500 + 8,000 - 2,500$$
$$= £174,000$$

Therefore, the owner's equity at the end of 2008 is £174,000, which equals the closing net assets of the business.

Question

The owner of a business introduced new capital of €15,000 during the year and withdrew a monthly salary of €2,000. If the net assets at 1 January 2008 and 31 December 2008 were €85,000 and €73,000 respectively, what profit or loss was made by the business in 2008?

Answer

The 'changes in owners' equity' equation states that:

$$OE = OC + P \ (or - L) + NC - D, \ so$$
$$P \ (or - L) = OE - OC - NC + D$$
$$= €73,000 - 85,000 - 15,000 + 24,000 \ (€2,000 \times 12 \ months)$$
$$= -€3,000$$

Therefore, the business has made a loss of €3,000.

Question

The balance sheets of a business at 1 July 2008 and 30 June 2009 show net assets of £85,000 and £105,000 respectively. The profit for the year for this business is £15,000. The owner made regular cash drawings of £200.00 per month and also withdrew goods for her own personal use on several occasions during the year. On 1 May 2009 she won the National Lottery and put the whole of her winnings into the business as new capital. What is the amount by which the cost of goods withdrawn by the owner exceeds or falls short of the amount of her National Lottery win?

Answer

The 'changes in owners' equity' equation states that:

$$OE = OC + P \ (or - L) + NC - D$$

Break the drawings (D) into two parts: D1 = cash drawings, and D2 = goods withdrawals. So, the equation becomes:

$$OE = OC + P + NC - (D1 + D2), \text{ so}$$
$$NC - D2 = OE - OC - P + D1$$
$$= £105,000 - 85,000 - 15,000 + 2,400 \ (£200 \times 12 \text{ months})$$
$$= £7,400$$

Therefore, the goods withdrawn fall short of the National Lottery winnings by £7,400. Or, the new capital invested into the business (National Lottery winnings) exceeds the goods withdrawn by £7,400.

Question

Alan sets up a business. Before he actually sells anything he buys the following:

Motor vehicles	€2,000
Premises	€5,000
Goods for resale	€1,000

He did not pay in full for the goods for resale and still owes €400 for them. He borrowed €3,000 from a friend for the business. After the above transactions he has €100 cash in hand and €700 in the bank.

Calculate the owner's equity of the business.

Answer

Use the accounting equation:

$$Equity = Assets - Liabilities$$

Assets	€
Motor vehicles	2,000
Premises	5,000
Stock	1,000
Bank account	700
Cash	100
	8,800

Liabilities	
Loan	3,000
Trade creditor	400
	3,400

Equity = 8,800 − 3,400 = €5,400.

Question

The following table shows the cumulative effects of a succession of separate transactions on the assets and liabilities of a business.

Identify clearly and as fully as you can what transaction has taken place in each case. Do not copy out the table but use the reference letter for each transaction.

Transaction assets		A	B	C	D	E	F
	£000	£000	£000	£000	£000	£000	£000
Buildings	80	80	80	80	80	80	80
Equipment	78	78	88	88	88	88	88
Stocks	33	38	38	36	36	36	36
Trade debtors	42	42	42	42	42	31	31
Bank	14	14	11	14	10	21	18
	247	252	259	260	256	256	253
Liabilities & capital							
Capital	126	126	126	127	127	127	124
Loan	75	75	82	82	82	82	82
Trade creditors	46	51	51	51	47	47	47
	247	252	259	260	256	256	253

Notes:

1 Notice that 'capital' is dealt with as a single item (any profits or drawings will affect this balance).

2 There are two possible answers to transaction 'F'; try to identify both.

Answer

A Purchase of stock costing £5,000 on credit terms.

B Purchase of new equipment costing £10,000. This was partly financed by a loan of £7,000.

C Stocks costing £2,000 have been sold for cash of £3,000. The profit of £1,000 has been added to capital.

D Paid £4,000 to creditors.

E Received cash of £11,000 from debtors.

F Either (a) paid business expenses of £3,000 in cash, thus reducing profit;
   or   (b) proprietor withdrew £3,000 from the business.

Questions

Answers are at the end of this chapter.

Question 1

Dun Horse and Associates, a firm of real estate agents, had the following transactions represented during September:

1 Arranged a sale of an apartment building owned by a client. The commission for making the sales was $5,000, but this amount would not be received until 20 October.

2 Collected cash of $2,000 from trade debtor. The debtor originated in July from services rendered to a client.

3 Borrowed $60,000 from HSBC, to be repaid in three months.

4 Collected $1,500 from a doctor to whom Black Horse and Associates rented part of its building. This amount represented rent for the months September, October and November.

5 The owners of Dun Horse and Associates invested an additional $10,000 cash in the business.

Required
Which of the above transactions represented revenue earned to the firm during the month of September?

Question 2

A business had the following transactions, among others during May:

1 Paid $2,000 salary to a sales representative for time worked during May.

2 Paid $500 for petrol purchased for the delivery van during May.

3 Purchased a computer for $2,500 cash.

4 Paid $14,000 in settlement of a loan obtained three months earlier.

5 The owner withdrew $400 from the business for personal use.

6 Paid $500 commission to a salesman for work performed last March.

Required
Which of the above transactions represented expenses incurred for January?

Question 3

Indicate the effect of each of the following transactions upon the total assets of a business by using one of the appropriate phrases as below:

> 'increase total assets'; or,
> 'decrease total assets'; or,
> 'no change to total assets'.

a Owner contributed a computer to the business.

b Purchased a motor vehicle for cash.

c Purchased a motor vehicle on credit.

d Paid a creditor amount owing.

e Received payment from a debtor.

f Purchased land for $100,000 paying $20,000 deposit and arranging a mortgage for the balance.

g Sold equipment for an amount of cash less than its cost.

h Sold equipment for an amount of cash greater than its cost.

i Received $260 from a debtor after allowing a $40 discount.

Question 4

1 The owner's equity of Sean Connery is $150,000 and is equal to one-quarter the amount of total assets. What is the amount of liabilities?

2 The assets of Pierce Brosnan amount to $60,000 on 30/6/20x7 but increased by $35,000 by 30/6/20x8. During the same year, liabilities decreased by $5,000 and drawings amounted to $10,000. If the owner's equity at 30/6/20x7 was $20,000, then what was the profit for the year ended 30/6/20x8 and the owner's equity as at 30/6/20x8?

3 On 30/6/20x8, the assets of Daniel Craig were $75,000. One year later the assets had increased to $100,000 and the owner's equity was $55,000. Liabilities were $20,000 greater on 30/6/20x9 than they had been at 30/6/20x8. What was the owner's equity at 30/6/20x8?

Question 5

Study carefully the following balance sheet and state the transactions that resulted in each change.

LondonCarRental Ltd
Balance sheet

	as at 03.03.20x9 €	€	as at 04.03.20x9 €	€	as at 05.03.20x9 €	€	as at 06.03.20x9 €	€	as at 07.03.20x9 €	€	as at 08.03.20x9 €	€
Current assets												
Bank	700		200		–		4,000		2,000		1,500	
Debtors	1,050		1,050		1,050		1,050		1,050		1,050	
Stock	5,900	7,650	5,900	7,150	5,900	6,950	5,900	10,950	5,900	8,950	5,900	8,450
Fixed assets												
Land and buildings	45,000		45,000		45,000		45,000		45,000		45,000	
Office equipment	3,500	48,500	3,500	48,500	4,000	49,000	4,000	49,000	8,000	53,000	8,000	53,000
Current liabilities												
Bank	–		–		300		–		–		–	
Creditors	1,500	1,500	1,000	1,000	1,000	1,300	1,000	1,000	3,000	3,000	3,000	3,000
Non-current liabilities												
Mortgage on land and buildings		40,000		40,000		40,000		40,000		40,000		40,000
		14,650		14,650		14,650		18,950		18,950		18,450
Owner's equity												
Capital		14,650		14,650		14,650		18,950		18,950		18,950
less: Drawings		–		–		–		–		–		500
		14,650		14,650		14,650		18,950		18,950		18,450

Question 6

You are given the following information for a retailer, George Michael, as at 30/6/20x8:

Capital as 1/7/20x7	$22,800
Cash at bank	4,000
Trade debtors	12,000
Accrued expenses	2,000
Trade creditors	10,000
Stock on hand	16,000
Buildings	16,000
Mortgage on buildings	8,000

During the past year George Michael has withdrawn $2,000 cash for his own use, while the net profit, according to the profit and loss account, was $7,200.

Required

From the above information prepare a balance sheet of the retailer, George Michael, as at 30/6/20x8.

Question 7

On 31 October 20x8, Mobile Centre Ltd, owned by Alex Ferguson, had the following assets and liabilities:

Cash on hand $200; bank overdraft $12,000
Land and buildings $100,000
Trade debtors $19,000
Mortgage loan $44,000
Trade creditors $15,000
Bank loan (due December 20x8) $3,000
Stock of stationery $500
Motor vehicles $28,000
Office equipment $4,500
Office furniture $1,800

Required

Prepare a balance sheet as at 31 October 20x8. Use the blank balance sheet provided below.

Mobile Centre Ltd
Balance sheet as at 31 October 20x8

Assets	$	$
Current assets:		
Non-current assets:	_____	
Total assets	_____	_____
Liabilities		_____
Current liabilities		
Non-current liabilities	_____	
Total liabilities		_____
Net assets		_____
Owner's equity		═══════
Capital – Alex Ferguson		_____

Question 8

Twelve months ago Linda Evangelista decided that she wanted to grow grapes and eventually produce wine. The business is called The Model's Vineyard Ltd and the transactions below are for the year ending 30 June 20x3.

Transactions:

20x3

Jul.   2   An account in the name of the business was opened and an amount of cash capital deposited.

Sept. 15   Purchased land and sheds for $125,000 paying $35,000 cash as the deposit and a mortgage from the bank for the balance. Repayments to the bank are to begin in one year's time.

Nov. 21   Equipment including a tractor and farming implements were purchased for $28,000 cash.

Mar. 14   Purchased an additional tractor paying $10,000 cash.

Jun. 11   Purchased farm supplies including fertiliser and minerals totalling $8,000 and paid with a cheque.

       30   The balance of the bank account is $49,000.

Required

Prepare a balance sheet for The Model's Vineyard Ltd as at 30 June 20x3 and calculate the amount of capital deposited on 1 June.

Use the blank balance sheet provided below.

The Model's Vineyard Ltd
Balance sheet
as at 30 June 20x3

Assets – Liabilities

Bank

Land & sheds

Farm equipment   _____

Farm supplies   _____

                                  _____

Mortgage

Net assets

Owner's equity

   Capital, Linda Evangelista

Question 9

Harrison Ford is the owner of Fine Artist Ltd and during November the following transactions occurred:

Nov. 12 Harrison Ford started business by depositing £23,000 into a business bank account.

5 Borrowed £30,000 from the bank to purchase shop premises. Purchased premises the same day.

8 Bought shop fittings for £3,000 – paid by cheque.

10 Purchased stock for resale, £5,500 on credit from his major supplier.

13 Sold £3,000 of stock for £3,000 cash.

16 Paid £2,500 cash into the business bank account.

18 Bought office equipment for £3,500 – paid by cheque.

21 Bought office furniture for £9,500 – paid by cheque.

24 Paid by cheque for £4,000 to his supplier as part settlement of the account.

26 Repaid by cheque £15,000 of the loan raised by the bank on 5 November.

29 Harrison Ford won £5,000 in a lottery and paid this cheque into his business bank account.

30 Sold £800 of stock to a customer for £800, on credit.

Required

Prepare a balance sheet for Harrison Ford as at 30 November. Use the blank balance sheet provided below.

Balance sheet as at 30 November

£   £

Question 10

David Bowie, a sole trader, has extracted the following trial balance as at 31 January 20x7.

Trial balance as at 31 January 20x7

	£	£
Telephone and internet	1,000	
Freehold land and buildings	29,500	
Cash in hand	100	
Purchases	65,000	
Trade debtors	8,100	
Sales		92,000
Salaries	15,200	
Trade creditors		1,900
Motor van	12,200	
Cash at bank	3,900	
Capital (as at 1 January 2007)		52,700
Rent	7,200	
Insurances	600	
Fixtures and fittings	3,800	
	146,600	146,600

Required

1 Prepare the profit and loss accounts for the year ended 31 January 20x7.

2 Prepare the balance sheet as at that date.

Use the blank sheets provided below.

Profit and loss account for month of January

Balance sheet as at 30 January 2007

Question 11

The following transactions are for Drew Barrymore who began a business called Hollywood's Acting Training Ltd. The business began on 1 July 20x4 and has been operating for one month.

Transactions:

20x4

July 1 The owner opened an account in the name of the business, depositing $67,000 in cash.

8 The owner purchased a bus to allow picking up young students. She paid $45,000 in cash for the vehicle.

18 Equipment was purchased on credit on 30-day terms. The cost of equipment was $7,500.

24 A student, Alison Ford, was invoiced for training services totalling $5,500. A loan for $10,000 was obtained from Barclay's bank to be used for the purchase of equipment at a later date.

31 An amount of $4,000 is received from Alison Ford as part payment of her account. Also, a payment of $3,000 was made on the equipment purchased on 18 July.

Required

Prepare a balance sheet for Hollywood's Acting Training Ltd as at 31 July 20x4. Use the blank balance sheet provided below.

Hollywood's Acting Training Ltd
Balance sheet as at 31 July 20x4

Assets – Liabilities

Bank
Motor vehicle
Equipment
Trade debtor _____
_____

Loan
Trade creditors _____
_____

Net assets

Owner's equity
Capital, Drew Barrymore _____
_____
_____

Question 12

The following transactions relate to the Aston Products Ltd, owned by Al Pacino:

20x6
June 1 Commenced business with: Cash $2,000; Vehicle $3,000; Land and buildings $35,000; Office furniture $800; Shop fixture and fittings $3,000; Stock $10,000; Mortgage on land and buildings $30,000; and Loan from Coventry Building Society $12,000.
2 Bought a van from Allen Ford – paid a deposit of $1,000. The remaining $4,000 was financed by HFI Finance Ltd.
3 Pacino withdrew $100 from the business bank account for personal use.
4 Paid $2,000 off the loan from Coventry Building Society.
5 Purchased office furniture for $750.
6 Purchased shop fittings for $340.
7 Raised short-term bank loan of $3,000.
8 Paid creditors $150.
9 Pacino contributed another vehicle worth $5,000 and cash $2,500 to the business.
10 Reduced the mortgage by $3,000.

Required
Present the balance sheet at the completion of the above transactions.

Question 13

Enrique Inglesias, a sole trader, extracted the following trial balance from his books at the close of business on 31 July 2009:

	Dr £	Cr £
Purchases and sales	6,500	12,870
Capital 1 Aug. 2008		2,470
Bank		1,430
Cash	50	
Discounts allowed and received	480	330
Returns inwards	250	
Returns outwards		190
Rent, rates and insurance	650	
Fixtures and fittings	3,800	
Delivery van	900	
Debtors and creditors	3,970	2,540
Wages and salaries	3,030	
General office expenses	200	
	19,830	19,830

Required

1 Prepare the profit and loss accounts for the year ended 31 July 2009.

2 Prepare the balance sheet as at that date.

Answers

Question 1

Requirement 1
Revenue of $5,000 has been earned in September.

Requirement 2
Revenue of $2,000 was earned in April. The cash receipt in September represents payment of that debt.

Requirement 3
The $60,000 represents a liability.

Requirement 4
Revenue of $500 has been earned in September. The remaining $1,000 would be recorded as rent received in advance (or unearned revenue).

Requirement 5
The $10,000 represents additional capital to the business and not revenue earned.

Question 2

Requirement 1
Expense of $2,000 has been incurred in May.

Requirement 2
Expense of $500 has been incurred in May.

Requirement 3
The $2,500 represents the purchase of an asset. The depreciation expense on the computer would need to be calculated for May.

Requirement 4
The $14,000 represents repayment of a liability. Any interest on the loan incurred for May would be expensed.

Requirement 5
The $400 represents a reduction in the owner's equity.

Requirement 6
The $500 represents the cash payment of an expense that incurred in March. It, therefore, only represents repayment of a debt for May.

Question 3

Requirement 1

a Increase

b No change

c Increase

d Decrease

e No chang

f Increase

g Decrease

h Increase

i Decrease

Question 4

Requirement 1
Liabilities = $450,000

Requirement 2
Profit = $50,000
Owner's equity = $60,000

Requirement 3
Owner's equity = $50,000

Question 5

Requirement 1
20x9
March 4   Paid creditors €500.
        5   Bought €500 of office equipment for cash.
        6   The owner(s) contributed €4,300 to the business.
        7   Bought €4,000 of office equipment, paying €2,000 cash and the balance on credit.
        8   The owner(s) withdrew €500 for personal use.

Question 6

Requirement 1

George Michael
Retailer
Balance sheet as at 30/6/20x8

Assets			
Cash at Bank	4,000		
Trade Debtors	12,000		
Stock on Hand	16,000		
Buildings	16,000	48,000	
Less			
Liabilities			
Accrued expenses	2,000		
Trade creditors	10,000		
Mortgage	8,000	(20,000)	
Net assets			28,000
Equity			
Capital 1/7/20x7	22,800		
Plus Profits			
1/7/20x7–30/6/20x8	7,200		
	30,000		
Less Drawings	(2,000)		
Capital 30/6/20x8			28,000

Question 7

No solution is given for this question. Students should attempt to answer it themselves.

Question 8

Requirement 1

The Model's Vineyard Ltd
Balance sheet as at 30 June 20x3

Assets – Liabilities	
Bank	49,000
Land & sheds	125,000
Farm equipment	38,000
Farm supplies	8,000
	220,000
Mortgage	90,000
Net assets	130,000
Owner's equity	
Capital, Linda Evangelista	130,000

Because you are given the balance of the bank account on 30 June, you only need to show the assets purchased and the mortgage taken out. Capital can easily be determined as a balancing figure (i.e. $220,000 – $90,000).

Question 9

Requirement 1

Balance sheet as at 30 November

	£	£
Fixed assets		
Premises	30,000	
Shop fittings	3,000	
Office equipment	3,500	
Office furniture	9,500	46,000
Current assets		
Stock	1,700	
Cash	500	
Debtors	800	3,000
Current liabilities		
Bank overdraft*	4,500	
Creditors	1,500	6,000
Long-term liabilities		
Loan	15,000	15,000
Net assets		28,000
Capital (23,000 + 5,000)		28,000

* Bank: 23,000 + 30,000 – 30,000 – 3,000 + 2,500 – 3,500 – 9,500 – 4,000
    – 15,000 + 5,000 = (4,500)

Question 10

Requirement 1

Profit and loss account for month of January

Sales		92,000
Purchases		65,000
Gross profit		27,000
Expenses:		
Telephone and internet	1,000	
Salaries	15,200	
Rent	7,200	
Insurances	600	(24,000)
Net profit		3,000

Requirement 2

Balance sheet as at 30 January 2007

Fixed assets		
Land and buildings	29,500	
Motor vans	12,200	
Fixtures and fittings	3,800	45,500
Current assets		
Trade debtor	8,100	
Bank	3,900	
Cash	100	12,100
Current liabilities		
Trade creditors	1,900	1,900
		55,700
Capital		52,700
Profit for the year		3,000
		55,700

Question 11

No solution is given for this question. Students should attempt to answer it themselves.

Question 12

No solution is given for this question. Students should attempt to answer it themselves.

Question 13

Requirement 1

Enrique Inglesias
Profit and loss account for month of July

Sales	12,870	
Return inwards	(250)	12,620
Purchases	6,500	
Return outwards	(190)	(6,310)
Gross profit		6,310
Discounts received		330
Expenses:		
Discounts allowed	480	
Rent, rates, insurance	650	
Wages and salaries	3,030	
General expenses	200	(4,360)
Net profit		2,280

Requirement 2

Enrique Inglesias
Balance sheet as at 31 July

Fixed assets		
Motor vans	900	
Fixtures and fittings	3,800	4,700
Current assets		
Trade debtor	3,970	
Cash	50	4,020
Current liabilities		
Bank	1,430	
Trade creditors	2,540	3,970
		4,750
Capital		2,470
Profit for the year		2,280
		4,750

Chapter 2

Processing accounting information

This chapter covers briefly the following topics:

- Double entry bookkeeping and ledger accounts
- The debit and credit rules
- Recording transactions
- Balancing off the accounts
- Trial balance

Double entry bookkeeping and ledger accounts

Double entry bookkeeping is a set of conventions for recording business transactions in a book called the 'ledger'. The ledger is divided into sections called *accounts*. The 'accounts' are used to show the detailed increases and decreases in each financial statement item.

Double entry bookkeeping is based on the same idea as the accounting equation. Every accounting transaction entered must involve an equal alteration to *both* sides of the accounting equation. As a result, each transaction has two equal but opposite effects, and the double entry bookkeeping means to record the dual effects of each business transaction.

Each account is split into two halves:

- the *LEFT* half is called the *DEBIT* side (Dr)
- the *RIGHT* half is called the *CREDIT* side (Cr).

For that reason, identifying debits and credits is quite simple.

In a system of double entry bookkeeping, every accounting transaction must be entered in ledger accounts both as a debit and as an equal but opposite credit. The principal accounts are contained in a ledger called the nominal ledger.

When the total amount of money on the DEBIT side of an account is *greater* than that on the CREDIT side, the account is said to have a DEBIT BALANCE. Similarly, when the total amount of money on the CREDIT side of an account is *greater* than that on the DEBIT side, the account is said to have a CREDIT BALANCE.

An account which contains a DEBIT BALANCE represents either an ASSET or an EXPENSE.

An account with CREDIT BALANCE represents LIABILITY, CAPITAL or INCOME.

The debit and credit rules

The **debit and credit rules** in double entry bookkeeping are as follows:

an entry on the *DEBIT* side is:	an entry on the *CREDIT* side is:
– an **increase** in an ASSET, or EXPENSE	– an **increase** in a LIABILITY, CAPITAL, or INCOME
– or, a **decrease** in a LIABILITY, CAPITAL or INCOME	– or, a **decrease** in an ASSET, or EXPENSE

Recording transactions: the process

Step 1
Identify the transaction and specify each account affected by the transaction (asset, liability, owners' equity, revenue (income) or expense).

Step 2
Determine whether each account is increased or decreased by the transaction. Use the rules of debit and credit.

Step 3
Create the double entry based on the **debit and credit rules** as described above.

Balancing off the accounts

At suitable intervals, the entries in each ledger account are totalled and a balance is struck (also known as closing off the accounts). This process creates nil balances in all revenue and expense accounts for the commencement of the new accounting period, while all balance sheet accounts have balances that are carried down at the end of the accounting period and brought down in the new accounting period.

Trial balance

A trial balance lists all the accounts of a business, with their balances. It is divided between accounts with debit balances and accounts with credit balances.

The total of each balance must be the same (check by entering on the trial balance the balance of each account and then add each side).

The trial balance is used as a basis for preparing a profit and loss account and a balance sheet.

Questions

Question 1

The transactions below are for the business 'Consulting Services Ltd' owned by Jere Duckin. The business began on 1 September 20x8 and has been operating for one month. The following transactions took place in the month of September:

20x8

Sept. 2 The owner's initial investment for the business to commence was $85,000 cash.

7 A small shop costing $50,000 was purchased and was paid for with a cheque.

14 Office equipment costing $14,500 was purchased and paid for with cash.

19 Shop fittings and furniture which cost $5,600 were purchased on credit from Real Furniture Ltd.

28 A loan for $15,000 was obtained from a local branch of the NatWest Bank. The money was used to purchase a motor vehicle. The loan repayments begin on 1 December 2008.

30 Paid $3,000 to Real Furniture Ltd for the fittings and furniture purchased on 19 Sept.

Required

1 For each transaction identify the accounts that will be involved.

2 Use the blank T-accounts supplied below to enter each transaction. You do not need to enter dates.

Accounts involved with each transaction

Transaction number:	Account title (DEBIT)	Account title (CREDIT)
1		
2		
3		
4		
5		
6		

BANK

Question 2

Interflow Plumbing Services Ltd began operating from its head office in Birmingham three months ago. Transactions relating to these three months have been as follows:

20x7

Sept. 5 The owner, Simon Collin, invested £155,000 of his own money for the business.

13 He purchased a small office and warehouse for £145,000. A deposit of £35,000 was paid and a mortgage for the balance was taken out from HSBC.

28 Office furniture costing £24,000 was purchased from PC World Ltd on credit.

Oct.	5	Five vans were purchased from Motor Centre Ltd. Credit of £85,000 was arranged with the car company while the balance of the purchase cost, £29,000 was paid for with cash.
	20	A payment was made to PC World Ltd for £12,400.
Nov.	3	One van was sold to another business for £22,800 with an agreement for the payment to be made within two months.
	15	A bank overdraft facility for £25,000 was arranged with the local bank.
	21	Equipment was purchased for £27,000 and paid for with cash.
	29	Payment was made to PC World Ltd to settle the outstanding balance owed on the account.

Required

1 For each transaction identify the accounts that will be involved.

2 Use the following blank T-accounts to enter each transaction. You do not need to enter dates.

Accounts involved with each transaction

Transaction number:	Account title (DEBIT)	Account title (CREDIT)
1.		
2.		
3.		
4.		
5.		
6.		
7.		
8.		
9.		

BANK

Question 3

You employ a very inexperienced book-keeper who, since you started in business a few days ago, has recorded the following in your accounts:

Cash account

		£			£
1 Sept.	Capital	12,000	3 Sept.	Office furniture	700
7 Sept.	Machinery	1,000	16 Sept.	Office furniture	100
25 Sept.	Capital	2,000	16 Sept.	Strong Tools Ltd	4,550
			28 Sept.	Bank	3,500
			30 Sept.	Machinery	1,500

Capital account

1 Sept.	Cash	£12,000	25 Sept.	Cash	£2,000

Office furniture

16 Sept.	Cash	£100	3 Sept.	Cash	£700

Machinery

		£			
7 Sept.	Cash	1,000			
30 Sept.	Cash	1,500			

Tools

12 Sept.	LTS Ltd	£5,000			

Strong Tools Ltd

		£
12 Sept.	Tools	5,000
16 Sept.	Cash	4,550

Bank account

28 Sept.	Cash	£3,500

Required

1 Re-write the accounts as they *should* have been entered using the following blank T-accounts, and

2 Prepare a balance sheet as at 30 September from the information portrayed by the revised accounts. Use the blank balance sheet provided.

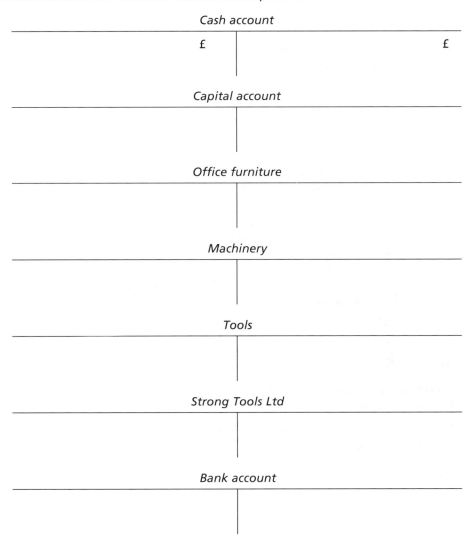

Cash account

£   £

Capital account

Office furniture

Machinery

Tools

Strong Tools Ltd

Bank account

Balance sheet as at 30 September

£

Fixed assets
Machinery
Office furniture
Tools

Current assets
Bank
Cash

Current liabilities
Creditors
Capital

_____

Question 4

1 Show the accounts involved in the transactions below under the main five headings of the financial statements (i.e. assets, liabilities, equity, revenue and expenses):

Modern Decorating Services Ltd

April 1   Brian Smith started business by investing $10,000 in cash.
       3   Purchased premises for $14,000 payable in ten equal annual instalments.
       4   Paid the first instalment from 3 May.
       4   Purchased $1,500 decorating supplies on credit.
       5   Paid wages $2,000.
       8   Received $8,000 for services sold.
       8   Invested a further $3,000 in the business.
     10   Bought a van for $2,000 cash.
     11   Sold services on credit for $4,000.
     12   Paid for the supplies from 4 May.
     15   Paid registration on van $300.
     16   Received $3,000 from clients from 11 May service.
     16   Withdrew $1,000 for own use.

2 Advise what accounts would be debited and credited.

Question 5

Show the general journal entries that are needed to record the following transactions of Johnson's Cleaning Services Ltd:

a The owner transferred $2,000 cash and a computer worth $5,000 to the business.
b Cleaning fees received $1,283.
c Purchased cleaning material on credit $766.
d Purchased cleaning tools $240.

e The business purchased cleaning equipment for $10,000, paid $2,500 by cheque and signed a one year, 12 percent loan payable for the remainder.

f Dry cleaning of uniforms $70.

g Paid wages $810.

h Drawings of cash by owner $200.

i Drawings of cleaning materials by owner $80.

j Cleaning fees invoiced $1,500.

Question 6

Even though a business's trial balance balanced, the following errors have been detected. You are required to prepare the correcting journal entries.

a A payment of $550 for rent was incorrectly recorded as $55.

b A $210 debt to rent was incorrectly debited to insurance.

c A receipt of $90 from an account customer was incorrectly recorded as a debit to trade creditors and credit to cash at bank.

d An invoice for $200 for fees had not been recorded.

e Cash drawings of $100 was incorrectly debited to the bank loan account.

Question 7

The trial balance of Copying Specialist Service Ltd as at 31 July 20x8 was as follows:

Copying Specialist Service Ltd Trial balance as at 31 July 20x8		
Account name	Debit ($)	Credit ($)
Cash at bank	22,000	
Trade debtors	7,000	
Photocopy supplies	700	
Equipment	15,000	
Motor vehicles	16,200	
Trade creditors		7,800
Capital		46,950
Drawings	250	
Photocopying fees		43,000
Supplies used	8,200	
Vehicle expenses	6,200	
Wages	18,000	
Office expenses	4,200	
	97,750	97,750

Transactions for the month of August were:

20x8

August	4	Purchased photocopy supplies $150.
	7	Cash fees for photocopying $50.
	12	Receipts from debtor $4,000.
	13	Billed customers for photocopying services $8,000.
	16	Cash fees for photocopying $80.

Paid fortnightly accounts:

vehicle expenses	$250
wages	$1,000
office expenses	$310

	18	Paid $7,000 owing to creditors.
	21	Purchased photocopy supplies $500.
	25	Cash fees for photocopying $110.
	26	Drawings by owner:

cash	$100
supplies	$40

	27	Billed customers for photocopying services $7,800.
	29	Paid fortnightly accounts:

vehicle expenses	$210
wages	$1,000
office expenses	$290

	30	Purchased photocopy supplies $600.
	31	Photocopying supplies used for the month $710.

Required

1 Record the above transactions in the general journal.

2 Prepare a trial balance as at 31 August 20x8.

Question 8

Five general ledger accounts are shown below in T-account format. Describe the transactions that took place following the recording of double entries.

Cash at bank			Purchases		
$		$	$		$
	(c)	760	(a) 1,000		

Trade creditors			Purchase returns		
$		$	$		$
(b) 200	(a)	1,000		(b)	200
(c) 800					

Discount received	
$	$
	(c) 40

Question 9

Below is a list of transactions for July 20x6 for Painting Jobs Done Ltd in its first month of operations:

20x6

July 1 Elton John invested $10,000 cash to start Painting Jobs Done Ltd. He also borrowed $5,000 from his bank as an interest-only loan for three years.

3 He rented a shop and paid $440 rent for the first month.

5 Purchased painting equipment for $2,800 cash and bought supplies on credit for $1,120.

6 Purchased a second-hand station wagon as a work vehicle for $5,500 cash.

8 Paid $550 in advance for newspaper advertising.

10 Billed clients $2,400 for completed work.

13 Billed clients for $900.

15 Paid $250 for telephone installation.

17 Received $500 from a client billed on 10 July.

20 Received $750 for a job completed today.

23 Paid wages of $1,180.

25 Paid creditors $720.

28 Withdrew $1,100 for his own use.

31 Found that $750 worth of supplies were still on hand.

Required

1 Record all transactions in the general journal.

2 Prepare a trial balance as at 31 July 20x6.

3 Prepare a profit and loss statement for the month.

4 Prepare a balance sheet as at 31 July 20x6.

Question 10

Dixens Ltd, a wholesaler of electrical equipment, starts business on 1 January with £100,000 in cash.

Jan. 2 Purchases warehouse for £35,000 and pays cash.

5 Purchases on credit stock of electrical equipment for £8,500 from CU Supplies Ltd.

7 Pays £25,000 cash into a business bank current account, and £5,500 into a business bank savings account.

9 Sales of electrical equipment for £6,100 and receives cash.

11 Pays advertising £1,140 by cheque.

13 Buys a second-hand motor van for £4,500 and pays by cheque. Original cost of van was £15,000.

14 Pays van tax £180 by cheque.
Pays insurance on van £350 by cheque.
Purchases petrol for £67 and pays cash.

17 Pays wages £500 in cash.

19 Purchases packing machinery for £940 and pays by cheque.

21 Sales on credit of electrical equipment to Small Electrical Shop Ltd for £3,100.

23 Purchases on credit stock of electrical equipment for £1,500 from CU Supplies Ltd.

25 Pays internet bill of £40 by cheque.

26 Pays wages in cash £450.

29 Sells on credit all remaining stock of electrical equipment for £8,500 to Dr X.

30 Pays general expenses of £1,000 in cash.

Required

1 Record all transactions in T-accounts.

2 Prepare a profit and loss statement for the month.

3 Prepare a balance sheet as at 31 January.

Question 11

A university graduate student has extracted the following trial balance.

Note: the *amounts* are correct per the ledger accounts, but entered under their incorrect headings of debit balances or credit balances.

Trial balance

	Dr £	Cr £
Capital		51,000
Premises	37,000	
Motor vehicles		8,000
Office equipment	4,000	
Sales		16,400
Purchases		9,200
Rates		1,100
Wages and salaries		4,100
Insurances	500	
General expenses	1,100	
Trade debtors		6,700
Trade creditors	5,000	
Advertising	700	
	48,300	96,500

Required

Re-draft the above trial balance showing the amounts of the various accounts under their correct headings of debit balances or credit balances.

Question 12

David Beckam, a sole trader, does not have any accounting background, but he has managed to extract the following trial balance from the books of his business as at 30 November 2009:

	Dr £	Cr £
Purchases	4,990	
General office expenses	990	
Bank overdraft	1,880	
Sales		10,880
Wages and salaries	1,880	
Cash in hand	90	
Sundry debtors	6,100	
Sundry creditors		1,990
Office furniture	2,900	
Capital account 1 December 2008		???
	18,830	12,870

Clearly, David is unable to ascertain the balance of the capital account at 1 December 2008. Also, there are obviously errors in the above trial balance, as all the *amounts* are correct per the ledger accounts, but some entered under the incorrect column.

Required

Re-draft the above trial balance showing the amounts of the various accounts under their correct headings of debit balances or credit balances, and insert the correct balance of the capital account as at 1 December 2008.

Answers

Question 1

Requirement 1

Accounts involved with each transaction

Transaction number:	Account title (DEBIT)	Account title (CREDIT)
1	Bank	Capital
2	Shop	Bank
3	Equipment	Bank
4	Fittings and furniture	Trade creditors
5	Motor vehicle	Loan
6	Trade creditors	Bank

Requirement 2

Capital – Jere Duckin

		$
	Bank	85,000

Bank

	$		$
Capital	85,000	Shop	50,000
		Equipment	14,500
		Trade creditors	3,000

Shop

	$	
Bank	50,000	

Office equipment

	$	
Bank	14,500	

Fittings and furniture

	$	
Trade creditors	5,600	

Loan

			$
		Motor vehicle	15,000

Trade creditors – Real Furniture Ltd

	$		$
Bank	3,000	Fittings and furniture	5,600

Motor vehicle

	$	
Loan	15,000	

Question 2

No solution is given for this question. Students should attempt to answer it themselves.

Question 3

Requirement 1

Cash account

		£			£
1 Sept.	Capital	12,000	3 Sept.	Office furniture	700
25 Sept.	Capital	2,000	7 Sept.	Machinery	1,000
			16 Sept.	Office furniture	100
			16 Sept.	Strong Tools Ltd	4,550
			28 Sept.	Bank	3,500
			30 Sept.	Machinery	1,500

Capital account

			1 Sept.	Cash	£12,000
			25 Sept.	Cash	£2,000

Office furniture

3 Sept.	Cash	£700
16 Sept.	Cash	£100

Machinery

		£
7 Sept.	Cash	1,000
30 Sept.	Cash	1,500

Tools

12 Sept.	LTS Ltd	£5,000

Strong Tools Ltd

		£			
16 Sept.	Cash	4,550	12 Sept.	Tools	5,000

Bank account

28 Sept.	Cash	£3,500

Requirement 2

Balance sheet as at 30 September

	£
Fixed assets	
Machinery	2,500
Office furniture	800
Tools	5,000
Current assets	
Bank	3,500
Cash	2,650
Current liabilities	
Creditors	450
	14,000
Capital	14,000

Question 4

Requirement 1

Current assets
Cash at bank
Trade debtors (or accounts receivable)
Decorating supplies

Fixed assets
Premises
Motor vehicles

Current liabilities
Trade creditors (or accounts payable)

Long-term liabilities
Loan

Owner's equity
Capital
Drawings

Revenue
Service fees

Expenses
Cost of supplies used
Van expenses
Wages

Requirement 2

April	1	Cash at bank (A)	Increase	Dr	$10,000
		Capital (E)	Increase	Cr	$10,000
	3	Premises (A)	Increase	Dr	$14,000
		Loan (L)	Increase	Cr	$14,000
	4	Loan (L)	Decrease	Dr	$1,400
		Cash at bank (A)	Decrease	Cr	$1,400
		Decorating supplies (A)	Increase	Dr	$1,500
		Trade creditors (L)	Increase	Cr	$1,500
	5	Wages (E)	Increase	Dr	$2,000
		Cash at bank (A)	Decrease	Cr	$2,000
	8	Cash at bank (A)	Increase	Dr	$8,000
		Service fees (R)	Increase	Cr	$8,000
		Cash at bank (A)	Increase	Dr	$3,000
		Capital (E)	Increase	Cr	$3,000
	10	Motor vehicles (A)	Increase	Dr	$2,000
		Cash at bank (A)	Decrease	Cr	$2,000
	11	Trade debtors (A)	Increase	Dr	$4,000
		Service fees (R)	Increase	Cr	$4,000
	12	Trade creditors (L)	Decrease	Dr	$1,500
		Cash at bank (A)	Decrease	Cr	$1,500
	15	Van expenses (E)	Increase	Dr	$300
		Cash at bank (A)	Decrease	Cr	$300

16	Cash at bank (A)	Increase	Dr	$3,000
	Trade debtors (A)	Decrease	Cr	$3,000
	Drawings (E)	Decrease	Dr	$1,000
	Cash at bank (A)	Decrease	Cr	$1,000

Question 5

Requirement 1

General journal

		Dr $	Cr $
a	Cash at bank	2,000	
	Computer equipment	5,000	
	Capital		7,000
b	Cash at bank	1,283	
	Cleaning fees		1,283
c	Stock of cleaning materials	766	
	Trade creditors		766
d	Cleaning tools	240	
	Cash at bank		240
e	Cleaning equipment	10,000	
	Cash at bank		2,500
	Loan		7,500
f	Dry cleaning	70	
	Cash at bank		70
g	Wages	810	
	Cash at bank		810
h	Drawings	200	
	Cash at bank		200
i	Drawings	80	
	Stock of cleaning materials		80
j	Trade debtors	1,500	
	Cleaning fees		1,500

Question 6

Requirement 1

General journal

		Dr	Cr
a	Rent	495	
	Cash at bank		495
b	Rent	210	
	Insurance		210
c	Cash at bank	180	
	Trade creditors		90
	Trade debtors		90
d	Trade debtors	200	
	Fees revenue		200
e	Drawings	100	
	Bank loan		100

Question 7

Requirement 1

No solution is given for this requirement. Students should attempt to answer it themselves.

Requirement 2

Copying Specialist Service Ltd Trial balance as at 31 August 20x8		
Account name	Debit ($)	Credit ($)
Cash at bank	15,930	
Trade debtors	18,800	
Photocopy supplies	1,200	
Equipment	15,000	
Motor vehicles	16,200	
Trade creditors		1,900
Capital		46,950
Drawings	390	
Photocopying fees		59,040
Supplies used	8,910	
Vehicle expenses	6,660	
Wages	20,000	
Office expenses	4,800	
	107,890	107,890

Question 8

Requirement 1
Goods to be placed in a shop as stock would have been bought on credit from a supplier. The source document would have been the supplier's invoice.

Requirement 2
Some of the goods originally purchased from the supplier have been returned reducing the amount payable.

Requirement 3
Payment of the outstanding balance to the trade creditor has occurred with $40 discount being allowed.

Question 9

Requirement 1

Painting Jobs Done Ltd		General journal	
20x6		$	$
July 11	Cash	10,000	
	Capital – Elton John		10,000
	Investment by owner		
	Cash	5,000	
	Bank loan		5,000
	Interest-only three-year loan		
3	Rent expense	440	
	Cash		440
	Shop rent for July		
5	Equipment	2,800	
	Cash		2,800
	Painting equipment purchased		
	Supplies	1,120	
	Creditors		1,120
	Supplies purchased on credit		
6	Motor vehicle	5,500	
	Cash		5,500
	Station wagon purchased		
8	Advertising expense	550	
	Cash		550
	Newspaper advertising		
10	Debtors	2,400	
	Sales		2,400
	Customers billed		
13	Debtors	900	
	Sales		900
	Customers billed		

Painting Jobs Done Ltd		General journal
20x6	$	$
15 Telephone expense	250	
Cash		250
Installation of telephone		
17 Cash	500	
Debtors		500
Debt received		
20 Cash	750	
Sales		750
Cash sale		
23 Wages expense	1,180	
Cash		1,180
Paid wages for month		
25 Creditors	720	
Cash		720
Paid creditor		
28 Drawings	1,100	
Cash		1,100
Monthly drawings		
31 Supplies expense	370	
Supplies		370
Supplies used for July		

Requirement 2

Painting Jobs Done Ltd
Trial balance as at 31 July 20x6

	Debit	Credit
Cash	3,710	
Debtors	2,800	
Supplies	750	
Equipment	2,800	
Motor vehicles	5,500	
Creditors		400
Bank loan		5,000
Capital – Elton John		10,000
Drawings	1,100	
Sales		4,050
Advertising expense	550	
Wages expense	1,180	
Supplies expense	370	
Telephone expense	250	
Rent expense	440	
	$19,450	$19,450

Requirement 3

Painting Jobs Done Ltd
Profit and loss statement for July 20x6

	$	$
Sales		4,050
Less Expenses		
Advertising	550	
Wages	1,180	
Supplies	370	
Telephone	250	
Rent	440	2,790
Net profit		1,260

Requirement 4

Painting Jobs Done Ltd
Balance sheet as at 31 July 20x6

	$	$
Assets		
Cash	3,710	
Debtors	2,800	
Supplies	750	
Equipment	2,800	
Motor vehicles	5,500	15,560
Liabilities		
Creditors	400	
Bank loan	5,000	5,400
Net assets		10,160
Owner's equity		
Capital – E. John	10,000	
Add Net profit	1,260	
	11,260	
Less Drawings	1,100	10,160

Question 10

Requirement 1

Students are advised to attempt the T-accounts first by themselves.

Capital

		£			£
30 Jan.	Balance c/d	100,000	1 Jan.	Cash	100,000
			1 Feb.	Balance b/d	100,000

Cash

		£			£
1 Jan.	Capital	100,000	2 Jan.	Premises	35,000
9 Jan.	Sales	6,100	7 Jan.	Bank	25,000
			7 Jan.	Bank savings	5,500
			14 Jan.	Van expenses	67
			17 Jan.	Wages	500
			26 Jan.	Wages	450
			30 Jan.	Gen. expenses	1,000
			30 Jan.	Balance c/d	38,583
		106,100			106,100
1 Feb.	Balance b/d	38,583			

Premises

		£			£
2 Jan.	Cash	35,000	30 Jan.	Balance c/d	35,000
1 Feb.	Balance b/d	35,000			

Trade creditor – CU Supplies Ltd

		£			£
30 Jan.	Balance c/d	10,000	5 Jan.	Purchases	8,500
			23 Jan.	Purchases	1,500
		10,000			10,000
			1 Feb.	Balance b/d	10,000

Bank savings

		£			£
7 Jan.	Cash	5,500	30 Jan.	Balance c/d	5,500
1 Feb.	Balance b/d	5,500			

Bank

		£			£
11 Jan.	Cash	25,000	11 Jan.	Advertising	1,140
			13 Jan.	Motor van	4,500
			14 Jan.	Van expenses	180
			14 Jan.	Van expenses	350
			19 Jan.	Machinery	940
			25 Jan.	Internet	40
			30 Jan.	Balance c/d	17,850
		25,000			25,000
1 Feb.	Balance b/d	17,850			

Motor vans

		£			£
13 Jan.	Bank	4,500	30 Jan.	Balance c/d	4,500
1 Feb.	Balance b/d	4,500			

Machinery

19 Jan.	Bank	940	30 Jan.	Balance c/d	940
1 Feb.	Balance b/d	940			

Trade debtor – Small Electrical Shop Ltd

21 Jan.	Sales	3,100	30 Jan.	Balance c/d	3,100
1 Feb.	Balance b/d	3,100			

Trade debtor – Dr X

29 Jan.	Sales	8,500	30 Jan.	Balance c/d	8,500
1 Feb.	Balance b/d	8,500			

Purchases

		£			£
5 Jan.	CU Supplies	8,500	30 Jan.	P&L a/c	10,000
23 Jan.	CU Supplies	1,500			
		10,000			10,000

Sales

		£			£
30 Jan.	P&L a/c	17,700	9 Jan.	Cash	6,100
			21 Jan.	Small Electrical Shop Ltd	3,100
			29 Jan.	Dr X	8,500
		17,700			17,700

Advertising

		£			£
11 Jan.	Bank	1,140	30 Jan.	P&L a/c	1,140

Van expenses

		£			£
14 Jan.	Cash	180	30 Jan.	P&L a/c	597
14 Jan.	Bank	350			
14 Jan.	Bank	67			
		597			597

Wages

		£			£
17 Jan.	Cash	500	30 Jan.	P&L a/c	950
26 Jan.	Cash	450			
		950			950

Internet

	£			£
25 Jan. Bank	<u>40</u>	30 Jan. P&L a/c		<u>40</u>

General expenses

	£			£
30 Jan. Cash	<u>1,000</u>	30 Jan. P&L a/c		<u>1,000</u>

Requirement 2

Profit and loss account for month of January

Sales		17,700
Purchases		<u>10,000</u>
Gross profit		7,700
Less expenses:		
Advertising	1,140	
Van expenses	597	
Wages	950	
Telephone	40	
General expenses	<u>1,000</u>	<u>3,727</u>
Net profit		<u>3,973</u>

Requirement 3

Balance sheet as at 31 January

	£	£
Fixed assets		
Premises	35,000	
Machinery	940	
Motor vans	<u>4,500</u>	40,440
Current assets		
Debtors	11,600	
Bank	17,850	
Bank savings	5,500	
Cash	<u>38,583</u>	73,533
Current liabilities		
Trade creditors	<u>10,000</u>	<u>10,000</u>
		103,973
Capital		100,000
Profit for the year		<u>3,973</u>
		<u>103,973</u>

Question 11

Requirement 1

Trial balance

	Dr £	Cr £
Capital		51,000
Premises	37,000	
Motor vehicles	8,000	
Office equipment	4,000	
Sales		16,400
Purchases	9,200	
Rates	1,100	
Wages and salaries	4,100	
Insurances	500	
General Expenses	1,100	
Trade debtors	6,700	
Trade creditors		5,000
Advertising	700	
	72,400	72,400

Question 12

No solution is given for this question. Students should attempt to answer it themselves.

Chapter 3

Accounting for stocks

This chapter covers briefly the following topics:

- The principles of stock valuation
- Stock valuation methods
- Overview

The principles of stock valuation

The need to value closing stocks arises from the *accruals/matching concept*. The cost of purchasing such stocks or goods arises in period 1, but if these stocks won't be sold by the end of the accounting period 1, then they will not produce revenue until these goods are sold in period 2. As a result, the cost of purchasing these stocks/goods in period 1 must be carried forward and charged against the revenue/profits in the later period (when they are sold).

The amount carried forward in this way should *normally* be the *cost* of the stocks. However, there are circumstances in which the *net realisable value* (NRV) of the goods will be lower than the cost, and in such cases the *lower of the two* is conservatively selected as the basis for the valuation of stock. In these instances, the lower-of-cost-or-market-value (LCM) method is used.

Lower-of-cost-or-market-value (LCM) method

Having identified the cost of closing stock, based on one of the stock valuation methods (see following section), the accountant has to undertake two further principal investigations which are concerned with the 'saleability' of the items contained in the closing stock figure. These are:

1 an examination of stock which is damaged, obsolete, or slow-moving;
2 an examination of what needs to be done (if anything) to make some of the stock saleable.

Under the LCM method (or rule), a market-price test is run whereas the *current market price (net realisable value* (NRV) – what you could sell it for) is *compared* with the *historical cost* derived under one of the three stock valuation methods (the figure currently shown in closing stock).

Under the LCM method, *the lower of the two* is conservatively selected as the basis for the valuation of stock. Thus, if the NRV is lower than the cost, then the accountant needs to *adjust the stock downwards*, and the NRV must be the amount shown in the accounts for that stock.

Remember that the accounting standards assert that 'provision is made for all known liabilities (expenses or losses), whether the amount of these is known with certainty, or is a best estimate in the light of the information available'.

Therefore, the adjustments made will take the form of a *provision* – in the interests of prudence and conservatism. In order to achieve the desired value of stock, an estimate of the amount of stock must be *written off*.

The bookkeeping is as follows:

Journal entries

provision for damaged (obsolete) stock	xxx
stock	xxx

The LCM method is an example of conservatism (prudence). Conservatism means selecting methods of measurement that yield lower net income, lower assets and lower shareholders' equity.

Example

Based on the historical cost and NRV figures of the following stock items, what will be the amount of closing stock shown in the balance sheet?

Stock item	Cost	NRV
A	1,200	1,000
B	1,000	1,100
C	850	600
	3,050	2,700

Answer:

Stock item	Cost	NRV	LCM method
A	1,200	1,000	1,000
B	1,000	1,100	1,000
C	850	600	600
	3,050	2,700	2,600

Therefore, the amount of closing stock shown in the balance sheet would be £2,600.

Stock valuation methods

There are two systems for keeping stock records: (1) the perpetual inventory system, and (2) the periodic inventory system.

The *perpetual inventory system* is a system that keeps a running, continuous record that tracks stocks and the cost of goods sold on a day-to-day basis. Thus, in the perpetual inventory system, the sale of an item and the accompanying inventory/stock reduction are simultaneous.

The *periodic inventory system* is a system in which the cost of goods sold is computed periodically by relying solely on *physical* counts without keeping day-to-day records of units sold or on hand. The following formula is used:

Opening stock (A) + Purchases (B) − Closing stock (C) = Cost of goods sold

where:

A + B = goods available for sale;
C = stock left over at the end of accounting year.

The amount of stock or goods sold during the year becomes an expense, labelled 'Cost of goods sold' or 'Cost of sales', and determines the gross profit in the profit and loss account.

The remaining (closing) stock held at the end of the accounting year, i.e. the stock or goods not sold by the end of the year, appears under the current assets in the balance sheet, and as such the remaining (closing) stock affects the financial position of a business.

Hence, it is very important that stocks be counted and valued correctly at the end of the accounting year.

Businesses purchase stock items or goods for resale frequently. When the stock is stored, different consignments that have arrived at different times during the same accounting year mingle together. Also, if the various consignments have been purchased at different unit prices, then it is *not* always possible to uniquely identify each stock item held at the end of an accounting period and to ascertain the cost of each item without difficulty. The question that is posed here is 'How do we know then which stocks were sold and which remain?'

There are three standard stock valuation methods used for determining the following:

- the cost of any stock sold or used during an accounting period;
- the cost of the closing stock held at the end of the accounting period.

These are:

1 *First in, first out (FIFO)*: using this method, we assume that components of stock or goods for resale are used in the order in which they are received from suppliers, i.e. we assume that the earlier stocks held are the first to be sold.

2 *Last in, first out* (*LIFO*): this involves the opposite assumption, so, using this method, we assume that the latest stocks held are the first to be sold.

3 *Weighted average cost* (*WAC*): using this method, we assume that purchase prices change with each new delivery of goods and, as a result, the average price of the stocks held is constantly changed too. Under this method, each batch of stock at any moment is assumed to have been purchased at the average price of *all* stocks held at that moment.

Overview

1 When the goods (products) are sold, the costs of the stock become an expense, labelled 'Cost of goods sold' or 'Cost of sales', in the profit and loss account. This expense is deducted from net sales to determine gross profit, and additional expenses are deducted from gross profit to determine net income.

2 If unit prices and costs did *not* fluctuate, all stock valuation methods would show identical results.

3 But prices do change, and these changes raise central issues regarding the cost of goods sold (income measurement) and the closing stock (asset measurement).

4 Stocks of goods purchased for resale are accounted for through the matching/accruals principle: the cost of an item should be deducted from the revenue it generates, so the costs of goods not sold in the year, i.e. closing stock, must be separated from the cost of goods sold in the year.

5 The higher the closing stock (and, hence, the lower the cost of goods sold), the higher the gross profit and vice versa.

6 The closing stock of year 1 will be the opening stock for year 2, so year 2's profit will also be affected by the valuation of closing stock in year 1.

7 The effect of the opening stock on gross profit is the opposite to the effect of closing stock on gross profit, since opening stock is added to the cost of goods sold.

8 So, the higher the opening stock, the lower the profit, and vice versa (compare with point 5 above).

9 The following formula can be used to calculate the *net purchases* made in the year. The net purchases appear in the 'cost of goods sold' account in the profit and loss account:

Purchases + Carriage inwards (or Freight-in) (CR) – Purchase returns (PR) – Purchase allowances (PA) – Purchase discounts (PD) = Net purchases where:

> CR = transportation (delivery) costs to move the goods from the supplier (seller) to the buyer;
>
> PR = unsuitable purchases (goods) returned to the supplier (seller);
>
> PA = when the buyer receives a deduction (an allowance) from the amount owed to the supplier;
>
> PD = when the buyer receives a deduction from the amount owed to the supplier by making an early payment to the supplier.

10 *Carriage outwards* (or Freight-out) is paid by the seller and is not part of the cost of the stock. Instead, carriage outwards is the expense of delivering goods to customers, and as such it appears in the operating (other) expenses in the profit and loss account.

11 The following formula can be used to compute net sales (see also pp. 96–97):

> Sales revenue – Sales returns and (any) allowances – Sales (trade) discounts = Net sales

Short questions

Question

Aston Ltd's stock valuation excludes a number of free samples from potential customers. They would normally cost £100 and could probably be sold to Aston Ltd's customers for £150. What is the effect on the company's profit of excluding this stock?

Answer

The profit is stated correctly, as it is correct to exclude free samples from the stock valuation. Besides, applying the LCM method, it is clear that the lower of cost and NRV is nil.

Question

Madonna's stock valuation includes certain damaged goods (clothes) at her original cost of £11,655. These could be repaired at a cost of £1,570 and sold for £12,150. What is the effect on Madonna's profit of including these clothes at cost?

Answer

The NRV of that stock is £10,580 (12,150 – 1,570) and, since the NRV is lower than the cost, the stock should be adjusted downwards and valued at £10,580 instead of £11,655. Hence, the effect of error is to overstate profit by that amount.

Question

The following details are taken from the books of Harrison Ford Ltd:

	¥		¥
Purchases	35,610	Opening stock	2,100
Returns inwards	990	Carriage outwards	2,990
Closing stock	4,870	Carriage inwards	1,430

Calculate the business's cost of goods sold

Answer

The calculation is:

Cost of goods sold = Opening stock + (Purchases + Carriage inwards) − Closing stock = 2,100 + (35,610 + 1,430) − 4,870 = ¥34,270

Note: return inwards are sales return and as such a reduction in sales, thus they do not affect the cost of goods sold. Carriage outwards is a distribution expense in the profit and loss account and is, therefore, unrelated to the above calculation.

Questions

Question 1

Suppose a division of a computer manufacturing company has these stock records for January 20x6:

Date	Item	Quantity	Unit cost (£)
Jan. 1	Opening stock	100 units	8
6	Purchase	60 units	9
21	Purchase	150 units	9
27	Purchase	90 units	10

Company accounting records reveal that operating expenses for January were £2,900, and sales of 310 units have generated sales revenue of £9,000.

Required

1 Prepare the January income statement, showing amounts for FIFO, LIFO and weighted-average cost (WAC). Label the bottom line 'Operating income'.

2 Suppose you are the financial accountant of that company. Which stock valuation method will you use if your motive is to

  a Minimise income taxes?

  b Report the highest operating income?

  c Report operating income between the extremes of FIFO and LIFO?

  d Report stock on the balance sheet at the most current cost?

  e Achieve the best measure of net income for the income statement?

State the reason for each of your answers.

Question 2

ABC Hardware Company began 20x4 with 60,000 units of stock that cost £36,000. During 20x4, ABC purchased goods on credit for £352,500 as follows:

Purchase 1	(100,000 units costing)	£65,000
Purchase 2	(270,000 units costing)	175,500
Purchase 3	(160,000 units costing)	112,000

Cash payments to suppliers totalled £330,000 during the year.

ABC's sales during 20x4 consisted of 520,000 units of stock for £660,000, all on credit. The company uses the FIFO stock valuation method.

Cash collections from customers were £650,000. Operating expenses totalled £240,500, of which ABC paid £211,000 in cash by the end of the accounting year. At 31 December, ABC accrued income tax expense at the rate of 35 percent of income before tax.

Required

1 Make summary journal entries to record ABC hardware's transactions for the year, assuming the company uses a perpetual inventory system.

2 Determine the FIFO cost of ABC's closing stock at 31 December 20x4 in two ways:

 a using a T-account
 b multiplying the number of units on hand by the unit cost.

3 Show how ABC would compute cost of goods sold for 20x4.

4 Prepare ABC Hardware's income statement for 20x4, including the calculation of the tax for the period.

Question 3

Calculate the missing income statement amounts for each of the following companies (amounts adapted and in millions):

Company	Net sales	Opening stock	Purchases	Closing stock	Cost of goods sold	Gross profit
Rainberry	£21,456	£(a)	£6,254	£1,399	£6,546	£(b)
Tasco	31,329	9,876	(c)	1,482	(d)	10,474
Safeone	18,726	768	3,453	241	(e)	10,063
Asca	(f)	433	1,325	(g)	997	2,995

Prepare the income statement for Asca, showing the computation of cost of goods sold. Asca's operating expenses for the year were £1,256, and its income tax rate was 31 percent.

Question 4

X Ltd, maker of DVDs and computer consumables, reported the following comparative income statement for the years ended 30 September 20x5 and 20x4:

X Ltd
Income statement
Years ended 30 September 20x5 and 20x4

		20x5		20x4
Sales revenue		£249,000		£222,000
Cost of goods sold:				
Opening stock	£18,000		£11,000	
Purchases	75,000		64,000	
Cost of goods available	93,000		75,000	
Closing stock	(19,000)		(18,000)	
Cost of goods sold		74,000		57,000
Gross profit		175,000		165,000
Operating expenses		130,000		123,000
Net profit		£45,000		£42,000

X Ltd's directors and shareholders are pleased by the company's increase in sales and net profit during 20x5. Then they discover that the closing stock of 20x4 was understated by £6,000.

Required
Prepare the corrected comparative income statement for the two-year period. How well did X Ltd really perform in 20x5, as compared with 20x4? What caused the evaluation of 20x5 to change so dramatically? Discuss in detail.

Question 5

Babycare accounting year ends each 31 January. Assume you are dealing with a single Babycare store in Leamington Spa, Warwickshire and that the following transactions need to be recorded: opening stock in 20x5 of 20,000 units that cost a total of £1,200,000. During the year the store purchased goods on credit as follows:

April (30,000 units @ £65)	£1,950,000
August (50,000 units @ £65)	3,250,000
November (90,000 units @ £70)	6,300,000
Total purchases	£11,500,000

Cash payments to suppliers during the year totalled £11,190,000.

During fiscal year 20x5, the store sold 180,000 units of goods for £16,400,000, of which £5,300,000 was for cash and the remaining was on credit. Babycare uses the LIFO stock valuation method.

Operating expenses for the year were £3,500,000, and the store paid 75 percent in cash and accrued the rest. Also, the store accrued income tax at the rate of 30 percent.

Required
1 Make summary journal entries to record the store's transactions for the year ended 31 January 20x5. Babycare uses the perpetual inventory method to record stocks.

2 Determine the closing stock based on LIFO stock valuation method using a T-account.

3 Prepare the store's income statement for the year ended 31 January 20x5.

Question 6

Silect Ltd, a fabric manufacturer, began March with 73 yards of fabric that cost £23 per yard. During the month, Silect made the following purchases:

March 4	113 yards @ £27
12	81 yards @ £29
19	167 yards @ £32
25	44 yards @ £35

At 31 March the closing stock consists of 60 yards of fabric.

Required

1 Determine the closing stock and cost-of-goods-sold amounts for March under (a) weighted-average cost, (b) FIFO and (c) LIFO.

2 Explain why the cost of goods sold is highest under LIFO. Be specific.

3 How much income tax would Silect save during the month by using LIFO versus FIFO? The income tax rate is 40 percent.

Question 7

Pizza Place's records include the following accounts with regards to purchases of plastic glasses as at 31 December of the current year:

Jan.	1	Opening balance (800 units @ £6.99)		5,592
	9	Purchase 300 units	@ £7.05	2,115
Mar.	23	Purchase 1,100 units	@ 7.35	8,085
June	12	Purchase 8,400 units	@ 7.50	63,000
Oct.	7	Purchase 500 units	@ 8.50	4,250

By 31 December the company sold 10,100 units for £154,876.

Required

1 Prepare a partial income statement though gross profit under the weighted-average, FIFO and LIFO methods. Use the periodic inventory system.

2 Which stock valuation method would you use to minimise income tax? Explain why this method causes the income tax to be the lowest.

Question 8

Dixens Ltd reported the following data (adapted in billions):

	2008	2007	2006
Net sales revenue	€37	€34	€31
Cost of goods sold:			
Opening stock	€4	€3	€2
Purchases	25	24	22
Cost of goods available	29	27	24
Less closing stock	(4)	(4)	(3)
Cost of goods sold	25	23	21
Gross profit	12	11	10
Total operating expenses	10	9	8
Net profit	€2	€2	€2

Assume that in early 2009, an error was discovered which involved the closing stock for 2006 being overstated by €1 billion and the closing stock for 2007 being understated by €1 billion. The closing stock at year-end 2008 was correct.

Required

1 Incorporate the above information and show corrected income statements for the three years.

2 Discuss whether each year's net profit as reported above and the related owners' equity amounts at the end of the year were understated or overstated. For each incorrect figure, indicate the amount of the understatement or overstatement.

3 How much did these assumed corrections add or take away from the Dixens total net profit over the three-year period? How did the corrections affect the trend of net profit?

Question 9

Fraser Department Stores Ltd operates a number of department stores in the United Kingdom. Assume that the company's accounting year ends each 31 January.

The store in London had an opening stock in year 20x0 of 55,000 units that cost £1,650,000. During the year the store purchases goods on credit as follows:

March (50,000 units @ £38)	£1,900,000
August (40,000 units @ £34.5)	1,380,000
October (180,000 units @ £35)	6,300,000
Total purchases	£9,580,000

Cash payments on credit during the year totalled £9,110,000.

During fiscal year 20x0, the store sold 285,000 units of merchandise for £14,000,000, of which £4,100,000 was for cash and the remaining was on account. Assume that Fraser uses the LIFO stock valuation method.

Operating expenses for the year were £3,180,000. Fraser paid two-thirds in cash and accrued the rest. The store accrued income tax at the rate of 32 percent.

Required

1 Make summary journal entries to record the store's transactions for the year ended 31 January 20x0. Fraser uses a perpetual inventory system to record stocks.

2 Determine the closing stock based on LIFO stock valuation method using a T-account.

3 Prepare the store's income statement for the year ended 31 January 20x0.

Question 10

Assume the H.A. Rod store in London began July with 50 (thousand) goods that cost £19.00 each. The sale price of each of these goods was £36.00. During July, H.A. Rod completed the following relevant stock transactions:

		Units (in £'000s)	Unit cost	Unit sale price
July 2	Purchase	12	£20.00	
10	Sale	27	19.00	36.00
13	Sale	23	19.00	36.00
	Sale	1	20.00	37.00
17	Purchase	24	20.00	
22	Sale	25	20.00	38.00
29	Purchase	24	21.00	

Required

1 The above information has been taken from the store's stock records. Which stock valuation method does H.A. Rod's use? How can you tell?

2 Determine the store's cost of goods sold for July. Also calculate the gross profit for July.

3 What is the cost of closing stock for the store at 31 March?

Question 11

Trade Cars Ltd had opening stock in February of 150 car wheels that cost £77.00 each. During February, the garage made the following purchases:

Feb. 2	222 @ £79.50
14	95 @ 82.00
19	210 @ 84.00
27	248 @ 87.00

Trade Cars Ltd's closing balance consists of 214 wheels.

Required

1 Calculate the closing stock and cost of goods sold amounts under the weighted-average cost (WAC), FIFO and LIFO stock valuation methods.

2 Discuss why cost of goods sold is highest under LIFO. Be specific.

3 How much income tax would Trade Cars Ltd save during February by using LIFO versus FIFO? The income tax rate is 31 percent.

Question 12

The records of Fordie Car Manufacturer Ltd include the following for a line of car exhausts at 31 March of the current year:

```
April   1   Balance  300 units @ €3.00 = 1,215
                      100 units @ €3.15 =
June    9   Purchase 800 units @  3.15 = 2,520
Aug. 21     Purchase 600 units @  3.35 = 2,010
Oct.  15    Purchase 400 units @  3.50 = 1,400
Dec.   8    Purchase 700 units @  3.70 = 2,590
```

The sales revenue generated during the year is £11,200.

Required

1 Prepare a partial income statement through gross profit under the weighted-average cost (WAC), FIFO and LIFO stock valuation methods. Use the cost-of-goods-sold model. Use the periodic inventory system.

2 Which stock valuation method would you use to report the highest net income? Explain why this method produces the highest reported income.

Question 13

The extract profit and loss account of Air Control Specialists Ltd is as follows (in millions):

(Amounts in millions)		2008		2007		2006
Net sales revenue		€1,517		€1,319		€1,238
Cost of goods sold:						
Opening stock	€269		€259		€234	
Purchases	859		729		663	
Cost of goods available	1,128		988		897	
Closing stock	(311)		(269)		(259)	
Cost of goods sold		817		719		638
Gross profit		700		600		600
Total operating expenses		500		450		420
Net profit		€200		€150		€180

Assume that in early 2009 it was discovered that the closing stock for 2006 was understated by £50 million and that the closing stock for 2007 was overstated by €20 million. The closing stock at 31 December 2008 was stated correctly.

Required

1 Incorporate the above information and show corrected income statements for the three years.

2 Discuss whether each year's net income as reported above and the related owners' equity amounts at the end of the year are understated or overstated. For each incorrect figure, indicate the amount of the understatement or overstatement.

3 How much did these assumed corrections add to, or take away from Air Control Specialists Ltd's total net profit over the three-year period? How did the corrections affect the trend of net profit?

Question 14

UK Airways Ltd is nearing the end of its first year of operations. The company made stock purchases of £745,000 during the year, as follows:

February	1,000 units @ £100.00 =	£100,000
May	4,000	121.25	485,000
August	1,000	160.00	160,000
Totals	6,000		£745,000

Sales for the year are 5,500 units for £1,500,000 of sales revenue. Expenses, other than cost of goods sold and income taxes, are £185,000. The directors of the company are undecided about whether to adopt the FIFO or the LIFO stock valuation method (assuming there is choice).

The company has storage capacity for 5,000 additional units of stock. Stock prices are expected to stay at £160.00 per unit for the next few months. The directors are considering purchasing 1,000 additional units of stock at £160.00 each before the end of the year. They wish to know how the purchase would affect net income under both FIFO and LIFO. The income tax rate is 31 percent.

Required

1 To aid company decision making, prepare income statements under FIFO and under LIFO, both *without* and *with* the year-end purchase of 1,000 units of stock at £160.00 per unit.

2 Compare net profits under FIFO *without* and *with* the year-end purchase. Make the same comparison under LIFO. Under which method does the year-end purchase have the greater effect on net profits?

3 Under which method can a year-end purchase be made in order to manage net profits?

Question 15

Assume a Parda factory outlet store began August 20x9 with 65 units of goods that cost £140 each. The sale price of these units was £270. During August, the store completed the following inventory transactions:

		Units	Unit cost	Unit sale price
August	2 Sale	16	£140	£270
	10 Purchase	80	141	
	13 Sale	34	140	270
	18 Sale	9	141	272
	22 Sale	35	141	272
	29 Purchase	18	142	
	31 Sale	10	141	272

Required

1 Determine the store's cost of goods sold for August under the periodic inventory system. Assume the FIFO stock valuation method.

2 Compute gross profit for August.

Question 16

Accounting records for The Best Pie Ltd include the following information for the year ended 31 December 20x8 (amounts in thousands):

Closing stock, 31 December 20x7	£390
Purchases of goods (on credit)	3,100
Sales of goods – 80 percent on credit; 20 percent for cash	4,500
Closing stock at the lower of FIFO cost or market value,	
31 December 20x8	610

Required

1 Journalise The Best Pie Ltd's stock transactions for the year under the periodic inventory system (show all amounts in thousands).

2 Report closing stock, sales, cost of goods sold and gross profit on the appropriate financial statement (amount in thousands). Show the calculation of cost of goods sold.

Question 17

You have found a source which can supply you with popular movies on DVDs at £2.50 each (normal retail price £7.99 and upwards). As a student, and being inexperienced, you see an opportunity of making some extra spending money by buying these DVDs and then re-selling them to your own family, friends and colleagues and to their friends. After some deliberation, you decide to purchase a supply of DVDs (at £2.50 each) and sell them at £4.50.

Over the next two weeks the following purchases and sales take place:

Week 1	No. of DVDs bought	No. of DVDs sold
Monday	20	
Tuesday		6
Wednesday	8	2
Thursday		3
Friday		7
Week 2		
Monday		10
Tuesday	15	4
Wednesday	19	
Thursday		6
Friday		4

Required

Calculate the profit or loss you have made in week 1 and week 2.

Answers

Question 1

Requirement 1

Income statement for component
Month ended 31 January 20x6

	FIFO		LIFO		Weighted average	
Sales revenue		£9,000		£9,000		£9,000
Cost of goods sold:						
Opening stock	£800		£ 800		£800	
Purchases	2,790		2,790		2,790	
Cost of goods available for sale	3,590		3,590		3,590	
Closing stock	(900)		(720)		(808)	
Cost of goods sold		2,690		2,870		2,782
Gross profit		6,310		6,130		6,218
Operating expenses		2,900		2,900		2,900
Operating income:		£3,410		£3,230		£3,318

Computations

Opening stock:	100 × £8	= £800
Purchases	(60 × £9) + (150 × £9) + (90 × £10) = £2,790	
Closing stock –		
FIFO:	90* × £10	= £900
LIFO:	90 × £8	= £720
Weighted average	90 × £8.975**	= £808 (rounded from £807.75)

* Number of units in closing stock = 100 + 60 + 150 + 90 − 310 = 90
** £3,590/400 units† = £8.975 per unit
† Number of units available = 100 + 60 + 150 + 90 = 400

Requirement 2

a Use LIFO to minimise income taxes. Operating income under LIFO is lowest when stock unit costs are *increasing*, as they are in this case (from £8 to £10). (If stock cost were *decreasing*, income under FIFO would be lowest.)

b Use FIFO to report the highest operating income. Income under FIFO is highest when stock unit costs are increasing, as in this situation.

c Use weighted-average cost (WAC) to report an operating income amount between the FIFO and LIFO extremes. This is true in this situation and in others when stock unit costs are increasing or decreasing.

d Use FIFO to report closing stock on the balance sheet at the most current cost. The oldest stock costs are expensed as cost of goods sold, leaving in closing stock the most recent (most current) costs of the period.

e Use LIFO to achieve the best measure of net income. LIFO produces the best matching of current expense with current revenue. The most recent (most current) stock costs are expensed as cost of goods sold.

Question 2

Requirement 1

Stock (£65,000 + £175,500 + £112,000)	352,500	
Trade creditors		352,500
Trade creditors	330,000	
Cash		330,000
Trade debtors	660,000	
Sales revenue		660,000
Cost of goods sold	339,500	
Stock		339,500
[£36,000 + £65,000 + £175,500		
+ £63,000 (90,000 units × £0.70)]		
(£112,000 ÷ 160,000 units = £0.70 per unit)		
Cash	650,000	
Trade debtors		650,000
Operating expenses	240,500	
Cash		211,000
Accrued expenses		29,500
Income tax expense	28,000	
Income tax payable		28,000
(£660,000 − £339,500 − £240,500) × 0.35 = £28,000		

Requirement 2

a Inventory		**b** Number of units in closing stock	
36,000	339,500	$(60,000 + 100,000 + 270,000 + 160,000 - 520,000)$	70,000
352,500	49,000	Unit cost of closing stock at FIFO	
	bal. c/d	$(£112,000 \div 160,000)$	$\times £0.70$
		FIFO cost of closing stock	£49,000

Requirement 3

Cost of goods sold:	
Opening stock	£36,000
Purchases	352,500
Cost of goods available for sale	388,500
Closing stock	(49,000)
Cost of goods sold	£339,500

Requirement 4

ABC Hardware Company
Income statement
Year ended 31 December 20x4

Sales revenue	£660,000
Cost of goods sold	339,500
Gross profit	320,500
Operating expenses	240,500
Income before tax	80,000
Income tax expense $(80,000 \times 35\%)$	28,000
Net income	£52,000

Question 3

Requirement 1

    a £1,691   (Let a = opening stock;
                  $a + £6,254 - £1,399 = £6,546$, so
                  $a = £1,691$)

    b £14,910 $(£21,456 - £6,546)$
    d £20,855 $(£31,329 - £10,474)$
    Note: must solve for d before determining c.
    c £12,461   (Let c = Net purchases;
                  $£9,876 + c - £1,482 = £20,855$
                  $c = £151,904$)
    e £8,663 $(£18,726 - £10,063)$
    f £3,992 $(£997 + £2,995)$
    g £761   (Let g = Closing stock;
                  $£433 + £1,325 - g = 997)$

Requirement 2

Asca
Income statement
Year ended 31 December 20xx

		(Millions)
Net sales		£3,992
Cost of goods sold:		
Opening stock	£433	
Net purchases	1,325	
Cost of goods available	1,758	
Closing stock	(761)	
Cost of goods sold		997
Gross profit		2,995
Operating expenses		1,256
Income before tax		1,739
Income tax expense (£1,739 × .31)		539
Net income		£1,200

Question 4

Requirement 1

After the adjustment and correction in the income statement, X Ltd actually has not performed as well in 20x5 as in 20x4, with net profits down from £48,000 to £39,000. The understatement of stock at the end of 20x4 caused 20x4 net profit to be understated. Then this same error caused 20x5 net profit to be overstated, giving the false impression that profits were higher in 20x5. In reality, net profit was down in 20x5 by £9,000.

X Ltd
Income statement
Year ended 30 September 20x5 and 20x4

	20x5		20x4	
	£		£	
Sales revenue		£249,000		£222,000
Cost of goods sold:				
Opening stock	24,000		11,000	
Net purchases	75,000		64,000	
Cost of goods available	99,000		75,000	
Closing stock	(19,000)		(24,000)*	
Cost of goods sold		80,000		51,000
Gross profit		169,000		171,000
Operating expenses		130,000		123,000
Net profit		£39,000		£48,000

* £18,000 + £6,000 = £24,000

Question 5

Requirement 1

Stock	11,500,000	
Trade creditors		11,500,000
Trade creditors	11,190,000	
Cash		11,190,000
Cash	5,300,000	
Trade debtors	11,100,000	
Sales revenue		16,400,000
Cost of goods sold	12,100,000	
Stock		12,100,000
[£6,300,000 + £3,250,000 + £1,950,000		
+ (10,000 units × £60*)]		
Operating expenses	3,500,000	
Cash (£3,500,000 × 0.75)		2,625,000
Accrued expenses (£3,500,000 × 0.25)		875,000
Income tax expense	240,000	
Accrued income tax		240,000
(£16,400,000 − £12,100,000 − £3,500,000)		
× 0.30 = £240,000		

* £1,200,000 / 20,000 units = £60 per unit

Requirement 2

Stock

Bal. b/d	1,200,000	COGS	12,100,000
Purchases	11,500,000	Bal. c/d	600,000

Requirement 3

Babycare Leamington Spa Store
Income statement
Year ended 31 January 20x5

Sales revenue	£16,400,000
Cost of goods sold	12,100,000
Gross profit	4,300,000
Operating expenses	3,500,000
Income before tax	800,000
Income tax expense (30%)	240,000
Net income	£560,000

Question 6

Requirement 1

Goods available for sale:

Opening stock	73 @ £23 =	£1,679	
Purchases:			
Mar. 4	113 @	27 =	3,051
12	81 @	29 =	2,349
19	167 @	32 =	5,344
25	44 @	35 =	1,540
Goods available	478		£13,963

a Weighted-average cost:

Closing stock: £13,963 / 478 = £29.21 per unit; 60 × £29.21 = £1,753
Cost of goods sold: £13,963 − £1,753 = £12,210

b FIFO cost:

Closing stock: (44 × £35) + (16 × £32) = £2,052
Cost of goods sold: £13,963 − £2,052 = £11,911

c LIFO cost:

Closing stock: (60 × £23) = £1,380
Cost of goods sold: £13,963 − £1,380 = £12,583

Requirement 2

The cost of goods sold for Silect Ltd is highest under LIFO because (a) the company's prices are not falling, and (b) LIFO assigns to cost of goods sold the cost of the latest stock purchases. When unit prices are rising, the latest stock prices are the highest, and that makes cost of goods sold the highest under LIFO.

Requirement 3

Cost of goods sold at LIFO	£12,583
Cost of goods sold at FIFO	11,911
Difference in cost of goods sold, gross profit, and income before tax	£672
Income tax rate	× 0.40
Income tax savings by using LIFO versus FIFO	£269

Question 7

Requirement 1

Pizza Place
Income statement
Year ended 31 December 20xX

	Weighted average		FIFO		LIFO	
Sales revenue		£154,876		£154,876		£154,876
Cost of goods sold:						
Opening stock	£5,592		£5,592		£5,592	
Purchases	77,450*		77,450*		77,450*	
Cost of goods available	83,042		83,042		83,042	
Closing stock	(7,480)		(8,000)		(7,002)	
Cost of goods sold		75,562		75,042		76,040
Gross profit		£79,314		£79,834		£78,836

* Total purchases = £77,450 (£2,115 + £8,085 + £63,000 + £4,250)
Computations of closing stock:
   Weighted average: £83,042 / 11,100 units = £7.48 per unit;
                      1,000 units @ £7.48 = £7,480
   FIFO: (500 @ £8.50) + (500 @ £7.50) = £8,000
   LIFO: (800 @ £6.99) + (200 @ £7.05) = £7,002

Requirement 2
When stock unit prices are not falling, then using the LIFO method minimises income tax, as the cost of goods sold is highest (gross profit is lowest).

Question 8

Requirement 1

Dixens Ltd
Income statement (adapted; *amounts in billions*)
Years ended 2008, 2007 and 2006

	2008		2007		2006	
Net sales revenue		€37		€34		€31
Cost of goods sold:						
Opening stock	€5		€2		€2	
Purchases	25		24		22	
Cost of goods available	30		26		24	
Closing stock	(4)		(5)		(2)	
Cost of goods sold		26		21		22
Gross profit		11		13		9
Operating expenses		10		9		8
Net profit		€1		€4		€1

Requirement 2

Net income and owner's equity effects of stock-counting errors:

Prior to correction of the error:	2008	2007	2006
Net profit for the year was	Over by €1 billion	Under by €2 billion	Over by €1 billion
Ending owner equity was*	Correct	Under by €1 billion	Over by €1 billion

* The profits are accumulated and carried forward each year.

Requirement 3

The corrections did not change total (accumulated) net profit over the three-year period. The corrections drastically altered the *trend* of net profit – from a smooth pattern (of €2 billion profits every year) to a sharp increase in 2007 (by €3 billion) followed by a sharp drop in 2008 (by €3 billion).

Question 9

No solution is given for this question. Students should attempt to answer it themselves.

Question 10

No solution is given for this question. Students should attempt to answer it themselves.

Question 11

No solution is given for this question. Students should attempt to answer it themselves.

Question 12

No solution is given for this question. Students should attempt to answer it themselves.

Question 13

No solution is given for this question. Students should attempt to answer it themselves.

Question 14

No solution is given for this question. Students should attempt to answer it themselves.

Question 15

Requirements 1 and 2

Periodic system

Cost of goods sold:

Opening stock (65 × £140)			£9,100
Purchases:	80 × £141 =	£11,280	
	18 × 142 =	2,556	13,836
Cost of goods available			22,936
Closing stock (FIFO)			
	41 × £141 =	£5,781	
	18 × 142 =	2,556	(8,337)
Cost of goods sold			£14,599
Sales	16 + 34 = 50 units × £270 =	£13,500	
	9 + 35 + 10 = 54 units × £272 =	14,688	£28,188
Cost of goods sold			14,599
Gross profit			£13,589

Question 16

No solution is given for this question. Students should attempt to answer it themselves.

Question 17

Requirement 1

Profit statement for weeks 1 and 2

			Week 1		Week 2	
		Workings:	£	£	£	£
Sales	*Week 1*	18 × £4.50		81		
	Week 2	24 × £4.50				108
Opening stock			–		25	
Purchases	*Week 1*	28 × £2.50	70			
	Week 2	34 × £2.50			85	
			70		110	
Less: Closing stock	*Week 1*	(28 – 18) × £2.50	25			
	Week 2	(44 – 24) × £2.50			50	
Cost of goods sold				45		60
Gross profit				36		48

Chapter 4

Fixed assets and depreciation

This chapter covers briefly the following topics:

- Depreciation of fixed assets
- The difference between capital and revenue expenditure
- Disposal of fixed assets

Depreciation of fixed assets

For some current assets (e.g. stock), their costs matched to the single period in which the associated revenues recognised. But:

what about assets that are not used up quickly (i.e. within a year)?

The cost of purchasing a fixed asset (e.g. machinery, buildings, etc) usually consists of a single, large payment. But the fixed assets produce revenues in numerous periods, and not just the one in which they are acquired. Hence, their costs must be spread across all those periods.

In other words, the fixed assets are used up, worn out or become obsolete (i.e. expire over time), and a process of allocating their costs of purchasing over time is applied:

- the allocation is called **depreciation** for tangible fixed assets (except natural resources);
- the allocation is called **depletion** for natural resources;
- the allocation is called **amortisation** for intangibles fixed assets.

No allocation (depreciation) is provided for the LAND.

Therefore, depreciation (or depletion or amortisation) is a process of spreading the original cost of a fixed asset over the accounting periods in which its benefit will be felt. Alternatively, depreciation is simply a system for cost allocation, or a systematic allocation of historical costs over the useful life of an asset. In other words, depreciation is the amount of a particular asset which has been used up over time as a result of being employed by the business.

Depreciation appears as an *expense* in the profit and loss account, and the annual charges are also accumulated in a *provision account* and taken in the balance sheet. The credit balance on this (provision for depreciation) account reflects the amount of the asset's original cost which has so far been written off.

In the balance sheet, the accumulated (or aggregated) depreciation on a fixed asset is deducted from its historical cost. The figure remaining is called the net book value (NBV) of the asset (or the written down value (WDV) of the asset), and represents the amount of its original cost which has not yet been written off (or it represents that portion of the cost of the asset which has *not* been treated as an expense yet).

When the purchase or sale of a fixed asset takes place in the middle of an accounting period, then the business accounting policy is normally applied, which is usually:

- full year's depreciation in the year of purchase and none in the year of sale, or
- depreciate asset from the month of purchase to the month of sale, or
- any other possible combination.

The annual depreciation charge on a fixed asset is based on three factors:

- The *depreciable value* (or amount) of the asset. This is the amount of the acquisition cost to be allocated as depreciation over the entire life of the asset. It is the difference between the total acquisition cost and the predicted residual value.

- The *estimated useful life* of the asset. This is the number of years before an asset wears out or becomes obsolete, whichever comes first (also known as economic life of the asset). This is normally measured in terms of years or in terms of units of service provided by the asset.

- The *residual value* of the asset. This is the amount predicted to be received from sale or disposal of a fixed asset at the end of its useful life (also known as disposal value, scrap value, salvage value or terminal value).

The most common methods of depreciation are:

- The *straight-line method*. This method spreads the depreciable value evenly over the total useful life of an asset.

  The annual depreciation expense that appears on the profit and loss account is:

$$\text{Depreciation expense} = \frac{\text{Acquisition cost} - \text{Residual value}}{\text{Years of useful life}}$$

  An *equal* amount of depreciation is charged for each year the asset is held, i.e. the depreciable value is spread *evenly* over the total useful life of an asset.

- The *reducing balance method*. This method applies a *fixed* percentage rate of depreciation to the net book value of an asset each year. To calculate the fixed percentage charge to be applied, we use the following formula:

$$P = \left(1 - \sqrt[n]{\frac{S}{C}}\right) \times 100$$

where: P = the fixed depreciation percentage (%);
$\quad\quad$ n = the useful life of the asset (in years);
$\quad\quad$ S = the residual value of the asset;
$\quad\quad$ C = the cost of the asset.

The annual amount of depreciation is calculated by applying the above fixed percentage rate to the cost of the asset, minus the accumulated depreciation of all previous years (i.e. the NBV at the start of each year).

Because the net book value is continually falling, the depreciation charge becomes *less* each year under the reducing balance method.

The bookkeeping for fixed assets is as follows:

Journal entries:

Dr	Fixed asset account
	Cr $\quad$ Bank (Cash or creditors)

Dr	Depreciation expense
	Cr $\quad$ Depreciation provision

The difference between capital and revenue expenditure

Asset-related expenditures (e.g. purchases of fixed assets, goods or services, whether for cash or on credit) can be capitalised (added to a fixed asset account) or expensed.

Expenditure with benefits extending beyond the current year should be *capitalised*, and transferred to the balance sheet – all other expenditure (i.e. those that provide a benefit lasting one year or less) should be *expensed*, and taken to the profit and loss account.

In other words, *capital expenditure* is expenditure on fixed assets and is included in the balance sheet of the business, whereas *revenue expenditure* is charged to the profit and loss account and relates to the running costs of the business.

In this way, the accrual/matching accounting concept is applied, whereas expenditures (costs) are initially capitalised, and then allocated in the form of depreciation (depletion or amortisation) over the periods the asset is used. This *matches expenses with the revenues produced*. In other words, it is an attempt to match the cost of the assets against the stream of revenues which the fixed assets help to generate.

Disposal of fixed assets

Fixed assets are not purchased by a business with the intention of re-selling them in the normal course of trade. However, the business will naturally dispose of them when their useful life is over, and may do so before then.

When an asset is disposed of, profits or losses on disposal are inevitable. But how are they measured? By taking the difference between the cash received (proceeds of sale) and the net book value (NBV) of the asset given up:

- if sales proceeds are greater than the NBV, a profit on disposal is made;

- if sales proceeds are less than the NBV, a loss on disposal is made.

The profit or loss on disposal is taken in the profit and loss account.

The bookkeeping for the disposal of a fixed asset is as follows:

> *Journal entries:*
> A disposal of fixed asset account is opened:

> Dr Cash (or bank or debtors)
>   Cr   Disposal of fixed assets

> Dr Disposal of fixed assets
>   Cr   Cost of fixed assets

> Dr Depreciation provision
>   Cr   Disposal of fixed assets

Finally, close down the disposal of fixed assets account by debiting (or crediting) the account. The balance on the disposal account now represents the profit or loss on disposal. If the disposal of fixed assets account is on the *credit balance*, then a profit on disposal is made; if the disposal of fixed assets account is on the *debit balance*, then a loss on disposal is made.

Short questions

Question

Indicate whether the following payments are 'capital expenditure' or 'revenue expenditure'.

1 Purchase of delivery van.
2 Payment of rent.
3 Payment of telephone bill.
4 Tax and insurance for van.
5 Repairs to machinery.
6 Decoration of office.
7 Purchase of machinery.

Answer

'Capital expenditure': 1 and 7.
'Revenue expenditure': 2, 3, 4, 5 and 6.

Question

Classify the following items as 'capital expenditure' or 'revenue expenditure'.

a   Wages paid to machine operators.
b   Installation costs of new production machine.
c   Rent paid for the factory.
d   Payment for computer time to operate a new stores control system.

Answer

'Capital expenditure': b*.
'Revenue expenditure': a, c and d.

* (b) Installation costs (and legal fees) are usually regarded as part of the cost of the asset.

Question

An asset costs ¥15,000, has a residual value of ¥1,000 and an estimated useful life of five years. Using the straight-line method of depreciation, what is the asset's net book value after one year?

Answer

Depreciable amount: ¥15,000 − ¥1,000 = ¥14,000
Annual depreciation charge: ¥14,000/5 = ¥2,800
Net book value after one year: 15,000 − 2,800 = ¥12,200

Question

An asset costs ¥15,000, has a residual value of ¥1,000 and an estimated useful life of five years. Using the straight-line method of depreciation, what is the asset's net book value after three years?

Answer

Depreciable amount: ¥15,000 − ¥1,000 = ¥14,000

Annual depreciation charge: ¥14,000/5 = ¥2,800

Net book value after one year: 15,000 − (2,800 × 3) = ¥6,600

Question

An asset costs ¥15,000, has a residual value of ¥1,000 and an estimated useful life of five years. Using the reducing balance method and a 40 percent rate per annum, what is the asset's net book value after one year?

Answer

Depreciation charge in the first year: ¥15,000 × 40% = ¥6,000

Net book value after one year: 15,000 − 6,000 = ¥9,000

Question

An asset costs ¥15,000, has a residual value of ¥1,000 and an estimated useful life of five years. Using the reducing balance method and a 40 percent rate per annum, what is the asset's net book value after three years?

Answer

Depreciation charge in the first year: ¥15,000 × 40% = ¥6,000

Net book value after one year: 15,000 − 6,000 = ¥9,000

Depreciation charge in the second year: ¥9,000 × 40% = ¥3,600

Net book value after two years: 9,000 − 3,600 = ¥5,400

Depreciation charge in the third year: ¥5,400 × 40% = ¥2,160

Net book value after three years: 5,400 − 2,160 = ¥3,240

Question

An asset costs ¥15,000, has a residual value of ¥1,000 and an estimated useful life of five years. Using the reducing balance method and a 40 percent rate per annum, what is the profit or loss made in the second year, if the asset is disposed of for ¥5,000?

Answer

Net book value after two years (see above): ¥5,400

So, loss on disposal of ¥400 is made.

Question

A small business has the following balances in its books as at 1 April 2007:

Motor vehicles (at cost)	$43,800
Provision for depreciation	$15,300

On 30 September 2007 one of the old vehicles, which was purchased for $12,000 (at cost) on 1 August 2005, was accepted in part exchange for a new vehicle

costing $14,000. The remaining balance of the cost on the new vehicle was settled through the cash account for $8,500.

The business's depreciation policy is 20 percent per annum using the straight-line method, with a full year's depreciation in the year of purchase, and none in the year of sale.

What is the balance sheet figure for the cost of motor vehicles and accumulated depreciation on motor vehicles at 31 March 2008?

Answer

Motor vehicles (at cost)

	$	$	
Balance b/d	43,800	12,000	disposal account
Bank	8,500		
Trade-in	5,500	45,800	balance c/d
	57,800	57,800	

Therefore, the balance sheet figure for the cost of motor vehicles is $45,800 at 31 March 2008.

Motor vehicles
Provision for depreciation

	$	$	
Disposal account		15,300	Balance b/d
$(2 \times 20\% \times \$12,000)$	4,800	9,160	Charge for the year
Balance c/d	19,660	–	$(\$45,800 \times 20\%)$
	24,460	24,460	

Therefore, the balance sheet figure for the accumulated depreciation on motor vehicles is $19,660 at 31 March 2008.

Question

The balance in the buildings account is €400,000 while the balance sheet shows the book value of the buildings at €217,600. The notes to the financial statements indicate that straight-line depreciation is used for all plant assets and that residual values are estimated at 5 percent of cost. The estimated life of the buildings is 25 years. What is the age of the asset in question, providing all assets were acquired at the beginning of the year?

Answer

€400,000 × 0.95 = €380,000 depreciable amount
€380,000/25 = €15,200 annual depreciation
€400,000 – €217,600 = €182,400 balance in accumulated depreciation
€182,400/€15,200 = 12 years old

Question

The following balances appeared in the balance sheet of Addax Limited at 31 March 2001:

	£
Plant and equipment – cost	840,000
Accumulated depreciation	370,000

In the year ended 31 March 2002 the following transactions took place:

1 Plant which cost £100,000 with a written down value of £40,000 was sold for £45,000 on 10 December.

2 New plant was purchased for £180,000 on 1 October 2001.

It is the policy of the company to charge depreciation at 10 percent per year on a straight-line basis, with a proportionate charge in the year of acquisition and no charge in the year of sale. None of the plant was over ten years old at 31 March 2001.

Prepare ledger accounts recording these transactions. A cash account is not required.

(From ACCA June 2002, paper 1.1.)

Answer

Plant and equipment – cost

2001		£	2001		£
1 Apr.	Balance b/d	840,000	10 Dec.	Disposal	100,000
2002			2002		
1 Oct.	Cash or bank	180,000	31 Mar.	Balance c/d	920,000

Plant and equipment – depreciation

2001		£	2001		£
10 Dec.	Disposal	60,000	1 Apr.	Balance b/d	370,000
2002			2002		
31 Mar.	Balance c/d	393,000	31 Mar.	Profit and loss a/c	
				(74,000 + 9,000)	83,000

Plant and equipment – disposal

2001		£	2001		£
10 Dec.	Plant & equipment – cost	100,000	10 Dec.	Depreciation	60,000
				Proceeds (cash or bank)	45,000
2002					
31 Mar.	Profit and loss account	5,000			

Questions

Question 1

Kayne West's accounting year-end is on 31 December. On 1 January 2007 he purchased a vehicle for £1,000 with an expected useful life of three years and an estimated residual value of £343.

Required

1 Calculate the amount of depreciation in each year of the asset's useful life using: (a) the straight-line method; and (b) the reducing balance method.

2 Show the double-entries relating to the depreciation expense, and the provision for depreciation in each year (using the amounts calculated from the straight-line method). Use the blank T-accounts provided below.

3 Show the double-entries relating to the depreciation expense, and the provision for depreciation in each year (using the amounts calculated from the reducing balance method). Use the blank T-accounts provided below.

4 Show the relevant balance sheet extract for 2008 (using the amounts calculated from the straight-line method).

5 Show the relevant balance sheet extract for 2008 (using the amounts calculated from the reducing balance method).

Requirement 2 (straight-line method)

Provision for depreciation on motor vehicles

Depreciation expense account

Requirement 3 (reducing balance method)

Provision for depreciation on motor vehicles

_____   _____

_____   _____

Depreciation expense account

_____   _____

_____   _____

Question 2

Frairy Ltd commenced business on 1 January 2006 with two vehicles – X and Y – costing £9,000 and £12,500 respectively. On 21 April 2007, vehicle X was written off in an accident and Frairy Ltd received £500 from the insurance company later in the year. On 1 May 2007 the business purchased another vehicle (vehicle H), which cost £15,000.

The business's policy is to charge a full year's depreciation in the year of acquisition and no depreciation in the year of disposal.

Required
Show the relevant profit and loss account and balance sheet extracts for the three years to 31/12/06, 31/12/07 and 31/12/08 assuming that:

1 The vehicles are depreciated at 20 percent on the straight-line method;

2 The vehicles are depreciated at 20 percent on the reducing balance method.

Question 3

Northeast Drycleaning Service Ltd has the following accounts on 31 May 2007:

	£
Machinery and plant	500,000
Provision for depreciation on motor vehicles	400,000

On 31 December 2007, half the machinery and plant was sold for £190,000 cash. The disposed machinery and plant was originally purchased on 1 January 2002. New machinery was purchased for cash on 20 April 2008 for £900,000. The machinery and plant are depreciated at 10 percent on the straight-line method. The business's policy is to charge a full year's depreciation in the year of acquisition and in the year of disposal, i.e. no allowance is made for parts of the year.

Required

1 Show the double-entries in Northeast Drycleaning Service Ltd relating to machinery and plant, depreciation expense, provision for depreciation, and disposal accounts. Use the blank T-accounts provided below.

2 Show the relevant balance sheet extract on 31 May 2008.

Machinery and plant

Machinery disposals

Provision for depreciation

Depreciation expense

Question 4

Mr Flo Rida owns a small factory and uses the reducing balance method of depreciation for plant, with a 60 percent write off each year, and maintains a plant account to record all entries concerning the plant.

An extract from the balance sheet as at 31 July 2008 is as follows:

Fixed asset	Cost	Depreciation	Net book value
	£	£	£
Plant	456,000	181,110	274,890

The plant T-account is as follows:

Plant A/c

2007		£	2007		£
1 Aug.	Cost balance b/d	391,000	1 Aug.	Provision for depreciation b/d	137,500
2008			2008		
30 Apr.	Provision for depreciation on plant sold	28,200	30 Apr.	Cost of plant sold	45,000
9 May	Assets purchased (at cost)	110,000	31 Jul.	Depreciation for the year	71,810
31 Jul.	Balance c/d	181,110	31 Jul.	Balance c/d	456,000
		710,310			710,310

Plant purchased on 19 February 2005 for £80,000 was sold for £1,250 on 10 November 2008.

New plant was purchased for cash on 16 June 2009 for £110,000.

The business's policy is to charge a full year's depreciation in the year of acquisition, but none in the year of sale.

Required

Show the double-entries relating to plant, depreciation expense, provision for depreciation, and disposal accounts for the year to 31 July 2009. Use the blank T-accounts provided below.

Plant account

Plant disposals account

Provision for depreciation of plant

Depreciation expense

Question 5

Britney Spears's accounting year-end is on 31 December. On 31 December 2008 her business had the following balances:

	£
Motor vehicles	50,000
Provision for depreciation on motor vehicles	24,500

Motor vehicles are depreciated using the straight-line method at a rate of 20 percent per annum and using the proportionate method of calculating the depreciation charge.
   The following transactions occurred during 2009:

- On 31 March, the business traded-in car A in part exchange for another car. The part exchange allowance on the car A was £3,750 and the balance of £5,250 was paid by cheque for the new car (car Z). Car A was originally bought on 1 April 2007 for £10,000 (at cost).
- On 1 May, the business purchased a van for £7,500.
- On 30 September, the business sold vehicle B for £5,100. It was originally bought on 30 June 2007 for £8,000 (at cost).

Required
Show the double-entries relating to the motor vehicles, depreciation expense, provision for depreciation and disposal accounts for 2009. Use the blank T-accounts provided below.

Vehicles – cost

Vehicles – provision for depreciation

_____|_____

      ——— | ———

Vehicles – depreciation expense

_____|_____

Vehicles – disposal

_____|_____

      ——— | ———

Question 6

The accounting year-end of Phillipps Ltd is on 31 May. On 31 May 2008 the business had the following balances on its motor vehicles account:

	£
Motor vehicles at cost	30,300
Less: Depreciation	7,100
Net book value	23,200

Motor vehicles are depreciated using the straight-line method at a rate of 20 percent per annum and using the proportionate method of calculating the depreciation charge in the year of acquisition, but no charge is made in the year of disposal. The profits or losses on the disposal account are written up on the last day of each accounting year.

The following transactions occurred during 2008–09:

- On 31 August, the business purchased a delivery truck for £10,300.

- On 30 September, the business purchased an estate car for a salesperson for £11,100. Also, the business sold a saloon car for £750 which was originally bought on 1 June 2004 for £3,150 (at cost).

- On 30 November, the business sold a minibus for £1,290 which was originally bought on 30 November 2005 for £9,800 (at cost).
- On 31 January, the business purchased a van for £9,900. The van was second-hand and originally cost £14,900.
- On 28 February, the business sold a pick-up truck for £1,680 which was originally bought on 1 March 2006 for £4,900 (at cost).

Required

Show the double entries relating to the motor vehicles, depreciation expense, provision for depreciation and disposal accounts.

Answers

Question 1

Requirement 1

a The straight-line method:

Annual depreciation: (£1,000 − 343)/3 = £219 per annum

b The reducing balance method:

Fixed percentage rate: $\left(1 - \sqrt[3]{\dfrac{343}{1,000}}\right) \times 100 = (1 - 0.70) \times 100 = 30$ percent

Annual depreciation:

For 2007:   30 percent of £1,000 = £300
For 2008:   30 percent of (£1,000 − 300) = £210
For 2009:   30 percent of [£1,000 − (£300 + £210)] = £147

Requirement 2 (straight-line method)

Provision for depreciation on motor vehicles

2007		£	2007		£
31 Dec.	Balance c/d	219	31 Dec.	Depreciation expense account	219
2008			2008		
31 Dec.	Balance c/d	438	1 Jan.	Balance b/d	219
			31 Dec.	Depreciation expense account	219
		438			438
2009			2009		
31 Dec.	Balance c/d	657	1 Jan.	Balance b/d	438
			31 Dec.	Depreciation expense account	219
		657			657
			2010		
			1 Jan.	Balance b/d	657

Depreciation expense account

2007		£	2007		£
31 Dec.	Depreciation on plant	219	31 Dec.	Profit and loss account	219
2008			2008		
31 Dec.	Depreciation on plant	219	31 Dec.	Profit and loss account	219
2009			2009		
31 Dec.	Depreciation on plant	219	31 Dec.	Profit and loss account	219

Requirement 3 (reducing balance method)

Provision for depreciation on motor vehicles

2007		£	2007		£
31 Dec.	Balance c/d	300	31 Dec.	Depreciation expense account	300
2008			2008		
31 Dec.	Balance c/d	510	1 Jan.	Balance b/d	300
			31 Dec.	Depreciation expense account	210
		510			510
2009			2009		
31 Dec.	Balance c/d	657	1 Jan.	Balance b/d	510
			31 Dec.	Depreciation expense account	147
		657			657
			2010		
			1 Jan.	Balance b/d	657

Depreciation expense account

2007		£	2007		£
31 Dec.	Depreciation on plant	300	31 Dec.	Profit and loss account	300
2008			2008		
31 Dec.	Depreciation on plant	210	31 Dec.	Profit and loss account	210
2009			2009		
31 Dec.	Depreciation on plant	147	31 Dec.	Profit and loss account	147

Requirement 4

Balance sheet at 31 December 2008 (using the straight-line method)

Fixed assets	£
Motor vehicles at cost	1,000
Less Accumulate depreciation	438
Net book value	562

Requirement 5

Balance sheet at 31 December 2008 (using the reducing balance method)

Fixed assets	£
Motor vehicles at cost	1,000
Less Accumulate depreciation	510
Net book value	490

Question 2

Requirement 1

Depreciation expense a/c:

2006

Vehicle X:	20% × £9,000 =	£1,800	
Vehicle Y:	20% × £12,500 =	£2,500	£4,300

2007

Vehicle Y:	20% × £12,500 =	£2,500	
Vehicle H:	20% × £15,000 =	£3,000	£5,500

2008

Vehicle Y:	20% × £12,500 =	£2,500	
Vehicle H:	20% × £15,000 =	£3,000	£5,500

Loss on disposal of X:

2007   (£9,000 − £1,800) − £500 = £6,700

Accumulated depreciation:

2006	£4,300
2007	£4,300 − 1,800 + £5,500 = £8,000
2008	£8,000 + £5,500 = £13,500

Frairy Ltd
Profit and loss account as at 31 December

	2006	2007	2008
	£	£	£
Depreciation expense	4,300	5,500	5,500
Loss on disposal of vehicle X	–	6,700	–

Frairy Ltd
Balance sheet as at 31 December

	2006	2007	2008
	£	£	£
Fixed assets			
Motor vehicles at cost	21,500	27,500	27,500
Less Accumulated depreciation	4,300	8,000	13,500
Net book value	17,200	19,500	14,000

Requirement 2

Depreciation expense a/c:
2006

Vehicle X:	20% × £9,000 =	£1,800	
Vehicle Y:	20% × £12,500 =	£2,500	£4,300

2007

Vehicle Y:	20% × (£12,500 – £2500) =	£2,000	
Vehicle H:	20% × £15,000 =	£3,000	£5,000

2008

Vehicle Y:	20% × (£12,500 – £2,500 – £2,000) =	£1,600	
Vehicle H:	20% × (£15,000 – £3,000) =	£2,400	£4,000

Loss on disposal of X:

2007   (£9,000 – £1,800) – £500 = £6,700

Accumulated depreciation:

2006	£4,300
2007	£4,300 – 1,800 + £5,000 = £7,500
2008	£7,500 + £4,000 = £11,500

Frairy Ltd
Profit and loss account as at 31 December

	2006	2007	2008
	£	£	£
Depreciation expense	4,300	5,000	4,000
Loss on disposal of vehicle X	–	6,700	–

Frairy Ltd
Balance sheet as at 31 December

	2006	2007	2008
	£	£	£
Fixed assets			
Motor vehicles at cost	21,500	27,500	27,500
Less Accumulated depreciation	4,300	7,500	11,500
Net book value	17,200	20,500	16,000

Question 3

Requirement 1

Machinery and plant

2007		£	2007		£
1 June	Balance b/d	500,000	31 Dec.	Disposals	250,000
2008			2008		
20 Apr.	Cash	900,000	31 May	Balance c/d	1,150,000
		1,400,000			1,400,000
1 Jun.	Balance b/d	1,150,000			

Machinery disposals

2007		£	2007		£
31 Dec.	Mach. and plant	250,000	31 Dec.	Cash	190,000
31 Dec.	Profit on sale	115,000	31 Dec.	Prov. for dep'n	175,000
		365,000			365,000

Provision for depreciation

2007		£	2007		£
31 Dec.	Disposals	175,000	1 Jun.	Balance b/d	400,000
2008			2008		
31 May	Balance b/d	340,000	31 May	Depreciation expense	115,000
		515,000			515,000
			1 Jun.	Balance b/d	340,000

Depreciation expense

2008		£	2008		£
31 May	Prov. for dep'n	115,000	31 May	P&L a/c	115,000

Requirement 2

Balance sheet as at 31 May 2008

Fixed assets	£
Machinery and plant (cost)	1,150,000
Less Accumulate depreciation	340,000
Net book value	810,000

Question 4

Requirement 1

Plant account

2008		£	2008		£
1 Aug.	Balance b/d	456,000	10 Nov.	Disposals a/c	80,000
2009			2009		
16 Jun.	Bank	110,000	31 Jul.	Balance c/d	486,000
		566,000			566,000
1 Aug.	Balance b/d	486,000			

Plant disposals account

2008		£	2008		£
10 Nov.	Plant	80,000	10 Nov.	Bank	1,250
			10 Nov.	Provision for dep'n	77,952
			10 Nov.	Loss on Sale	798
		80,000			80,000

Provision for depreciation of plant

2008		£	2008		£
4 Dec.	Disposals	77,952	1 Aug.	Balance b/d	181,110
2009			2009		
30 Sep.	Balance c/d	332,863	31 Jul.	Dep'n expense*	229,705
		410,815			410,815
			1 Aug.	Balance b/d	332,863

Depreciation expense

2009		£	2009		£
31 Jul.	Provision for dep'n*	229,705	31 Jul.	P&L a/c	163,705

* Depreciation expense for the year:
$(274,890 - 2,048) \times 60\% = 163,705$
$110,000 \times 60\% = \underline{\quad 66,000}$
$\underline{£229,705}$

Question 5

Requirement 1

Vehicle A – Depreciation on disposal:

For year ending 31/12/2007:

$20\% \times 10,000 \times 9/12 = \qquad 1,500$

For year ending 31/12/2008:

$20\% \times 10,000 \times 12/12 = \qquad 2,000$

For year ending 31/12/2009:

$20\% \times 10,000 \times 3/12 = \qquad \underline{\quad 500} \quad \underline{£4,000}$

Loss on sale of vehicle A: $(£10,000 - £4,000) - £3,750 = \underline{£2,250}$

Vehicle B – Depreciation on disposal:

For year ending 31/12/2007:

$20\% \times 8,000 \times 6/12 = \qquad 800$

For year ending 31/12/2008:

$20\% \times 8,000 \times 12/12 = \qquad 1,600$

For year ending 31/12/2009:

$20\% \times 8,000 \times 9/12 = \qquad \underline{1,200} \quad \underline{£3,600}$

Profit on sale of vehicle B: $(£8,000 - £3,600) - £5,100 = \underline{£700}$

Depreciation expense a/c for 2009:

Depreciation on disposals:
31.03.2009 – Vehicle A:	$20\% \times 10,000 \times 3/12 =$	500
30.09.2009 – Vehicle B:	$20\% \times 8,000 \times 9/12 =$	1,200

Depreciation on acquisitions:
31.03.2009 – Car Z:	$20\% \times (3,750 + 5,250) \times 9/12 =$	1,350
01.05.2009 – Van:	$20\% \times 7,500 \times 8/12 =$	1,000

Depreciation on remainder:
$20\% \times (50,000 - 10,000 - 8,000) = \qquad \underline{6,400} \quad \underline{£10,450}$

Vehicles – cost

2009		£	2009		£
1 Jan.	Balance b/d	50,000			
31 Mar.	Bank	5,250	31 Mar.	Disposal of car A	10,000
31 Mar.	Part exchange	3,750	30 Sep.	Disposal of car B	8,000
1 May	Bank	7,500	31 Dec.	Balance c/d	48,500
		66,500			25,800
2010					
1 Jan.	Balance b/d	48,500			

Vehicles – provision for depreciation

2009		£	2009		£
31 Mar.	Disposal of car A	4,000	1 Jan.	Balance b/d	24,500
30 Sep.	Disposal of car B	3,600	31 Dec.	Depreciation	
				expense	10,450
31 Dec.	Balance c/d	27,350			
		34,950			34,950
			2010		
			1 Jan.	Balance b/d	27,350

Vehicles – depreciation expense

2009		£	2009		£
31 Dec.	Provision for		31 Dec.	Profit and loss a/c	10,450
	depreciation	10,450			

Vehicles – disposal

2009		£	2009		£
31 Mar.	Vehicle A – cost	10,000	31 Mar.	Proceeds – part	
				exchange	3,750
30 Sep.	Vehicle B – cost	8,000	31 Mar.	Provision for	
				depreciation	4,000
			30 Sep.	Proceeds – bank	5,100
			30 Sep.	Provision for	
				depreciation	3,600
30 Sep.	Profit on disposal		31 Mar.	Loss on disposal	
	(car B)	700		(car A)	2,250
		18,700			18,700

Question 6

Requirement 1

Accumulated depreciation on disposals:

Saloon car	20% × £3,150 × 4 years =	2,520
Minibus	20% × £9,800 × 2 years 6 months =	4,900
Pick-up truck	20% × £4,900 × 2 years 3 months =	2,205
		9,625

Profit on sale of saloon car: $(3,150 - 2,520) - 750 =$ £120
Loss on sale of minibus: $(9,800 - 4,900) - 1,290 =$ £3,610
Loss on sale of pick-up truck: $(4,900 - 2,205) - 1,680 =$ £1,015

Depreciation expense a/c for 2009:

Depreciation on acquisitions:

31.08.08	Delivery truck	$20\% \times £10,300 \times 9/12$	1,545
30.09.08	Estate car	$20\% \times £11,100 \times 8/12$	1,480
31.01.09	Van	$20\% \times £9,900 \times 4/12$	660

Depreciation on remainder:

$20\% \times (£30,300 - £3,150 - £9,800 - £4,900)$ 2,490

6,175

Vehicles – cost

2008		£	2008		£
1 Jun.	Balance b/d	30,300	30 Sep.	Disposal of saloon car	3,150
31 Aug.	Bank	10,300	30 Nov.	Disposal of minibus	9,800
30 Sep.	Bank	11,100			
2009			2009		
31 Jan.	Bank	9,900	28 Feb.	Disposal of pick-up truck	4,900
			31 May	Balance c/d	43,750
		61,600			61,600
1 Jun.	Balance b/d	43,750			

Vehicles – provision for depreciation

2008		£	2008		£
30 Sep.	Disposal of saloon car	2,520	1 Jun.	Balance b/d	7,100
30 Nov.	Disposal of minibus	4,900			
2009			2009		
28 Feb.	Disposal of pick-up truck	2,205	31 May	Depreciation expense	6,175
31 May	Balance c/d	3,650			
		13,275			13,275
			1 Jun.	Balance b/d	3,650

Vehicles – depreciation expense

2009		£	2009		£
31 May	Provision for depreciation	6,175	31 May	Profit and loss a/c	6,175

Vehicles – disposal

2008		£	2008		£
30 Sep.	Saloon car – cost	3,150	30 Sep.	Proceeds – bank	750
30 Nov.	Minibus – cost	9,800	30 Sep.	Provision for depreciation	2,520
			30 Nov.	Proceeds – bank	1,290
			30 Nov.	Provision for depreciation	4,900
2009			2009		
28 Feb.	Pick-up truck – cost	4,900	28 Feb.	Proceeds – bank	1,680
			28 Feb.	Provision for depreciation	2,205
31 May	Profit on sale (saloon car)	120	31 May	Loss on disposal (minibus)	3,610
			31 May	Loss on disposal (pick-up truck)	1,015
		17,970			17,970

Chapter 5

Final adjustments to accounts

This chapter covers briefly the following topics:

- Accruals and prepayments
- Credit sales and discounts
- Bad debts and provision for doubtful debts
- Suspense accounts

Final adjustments are entered in the books of a business at the end of the accounting period in order to update or modify account balances. This is done so that the accounts are up to date when the financial statements are prepared. The adjustments being made at the end of the accounting period refer to accruals, prepayments, provision for doubtful debts and depreciation (see Chapter 4). We will also talk about credit sales and discounts, and suspense accounts.

Accruals and prepayments

The accruals concept or method recognises that revenues and costs are accrued (that is, recognised as they are earned or incurred, independent of the time when money/cash is paid or received).

The accruals concept is aligned with the matching principle, which attempts to match the revenue earned in a particular period with the expenses incurred in earning that revenue for that period. In other words, revenues and costs are matched with one another so far as their relationship can be established, and dealt with in the profit and loss account (income statement) of the period to which they relate.

The matching process would normally be a simple process if we could rely on the date of payment to indicate the date on which an expense is incurred. Unfortunately, there is often a difference between the date when an expense is incurred and the date it is paid.

There are two main reasons for this:

- Goods and services may be provided by suppliers on credit terms. Although the benefits may be enjoyed in period 1, payment may not be due until period 2. This difficulty is dealt with by the system of debtors and creditors accounts in the books of a business.

- Many expenses (such as an electricity bill) relate to services provided over an extended period (say, three months). The expenditure must be spread over the period during which the service was enjoyed, even though payment of course takes place on a single day. This difficulty is dealt with by the system of accruals and prepayments.

An accrual or an accrued expense refers to an expense that has been incurred in the accounting period, but no cash has been paid for it by the end of the accounting period. This expense needs to be recorded in the period it is incurred as does the business's liability for payment.

In other words, an accrual is an expense which has not yet been entered into an expense account because no invoice has been received at the year-end, hence it is an *expense* that needs to be charged to the current year *profit and loss account*. It is also a current liability at the year end (i.e. a creditor in the balance sheet), hence it is a *current liability* in the *balance sheet*.

For an *accrual* or an accrued expense, the *double entry* in a business's books is: debit the expense account with the amount owing at the end of the accounting period, and credit the accrual account.

In the next period, when the accrued amount owed is due and paid, the amount is posted to the debit of the accrual account, i.e. clear your current liability of accrual.

A prepayment or a prepaid expense refers to expenditure which is made in one accounting period covering a term which extends beyond the end of that period, i.e. cash is paid in advance before expenses have been incurred.

In other words, a prepayment is an expense which has already been entered in an expense account (because an invoice has been received) but which is not a part of expenditure relating to the current year, hence the amount paid must *not* be charged as an *expense* in the *profit and loss account*. It is a current asset at the year end, similar to a debtor, hence it is a *current asset* in the *balance sheet*.

When the invoice is received, the *double entry* in a business's books is: debit the expense account, and credit the bank or cash.

For a *prepayment* or a prepaid expense, the *double entry* in a business's books is: debit the prepayment account, and credit the expense account with the amount of prepayment.

In the next period, charge the profit and loss account with the amount of the prepayment brought forward from the last accounting period (by crediting the prepayment account).

Combined rules for accruals and prepayments

Instead of keeping separate accounts for accruals and prepayments (as indicated in the preceeding section), another approach brings together the expense accounts and the accruals and prepayments under one account.

The *accrual rule* of the *double entry* is as follows: debit the amount owing at the end of the year to the relevant expense account as a balance carried down and credit the same amount as a balance brought down.

Note that the amount transferred to the profit and loss account is the difference between the two sides of the combined expense (and accrual) account *after* entering the accrual at the end of the year (i.e. after entering the balance carried down on the debit side of the account).

Similarly, the *prepayment rule* of the *double entry* is as follows: credit the amount of the prepayment to the expense account as a balance carried down and debit the same amount as a balance brought down.

Note that the amount transferred to the profit and loss account is the difference between the two sides of the combined expense (and prepayment) account *after* entering the prepayment at the end of the year (i.e. after entering the balance carried down on the credit side of the account).

Credit sales and discounts

There are costs association with selling on credit: credit sales (receivables) are usually good for a business to have because they are claims to someone else's cash.

However, a receivable can be bad news if the business cannot collect the receivable. Accountants label this cost 'uncollectible-account expense', 'doubtful-account expense' or 'bad-debt expense'.

When credit sales take place, the *double entry* in business's books is: debit the trade debtors (trade receivables), and credit the sales account. When a cheque or cash is received by the customers (trade debtors), the *double entry* in business's books is: debit the bank or cash, and credit the trade debtors. When customers return goods sold to them back to the seller, the *double entry* in business's books is: debit the sales returns (sales inwards), and credit the trade debtors.

A discount given to customers is a reduction in the price of goods or services. A business may have a list price at which it is prepared to sell its goods or services to the majority of customers. However, there may be reasons which justify a lower price to certain particular customers or categories of customers. In such a case, the business is said to allow (or offer) a discount to these customers.

It is useful to distinguish between two classes of discount:

- *Cash discount* is granted to customers who are prepared to pay immediately in cash or by cheque, instead of purchasing on credit terms.
- *Settlement discount* is granted to credit customers who pay within a specified period from the invoice date, or as an incentive to make payment before the due date.

Cash discount and settlement discount are similar in nature. The object of both is to improve the business's cash flow by encouraging prompt (or, earlier) payment by customers. The cost of the discount to the business is in the nature of a financing charge, and this should be shown as an *expense* in the profit and loss account. *For cash discount*, the *double entry* in a business's books is: debit bank (or cash) and discount given (allowed), credit sales. *For settlement discount*, the *double entry* in a business's books is: debit discount given (allowed), credit trade debtors.

There is another class of discount, the trade discount which is granted to regular customers, usually those buying in bulk quantities. Trade discount is genuinely a reduction in the selling price made in order to attract a higher level of business. For this reason, it is accounted for as a reduction in the value of sales turnover. There is no double entry for trade discounts. The trade discount is deducted on the sale invoice in arriving at the amount that the seller will sell the goods for.

Finally, a business may be offered a discount by its suppliers to pay on time or before the due date, and this is referred to as discount received. Discount received is revenue (income) for a business, and the *double entry* in a business's books is: debit trade creditor (trade accounts payable), credit discount received.

Bad debts and provision for doubtful debts

For one reason or another, a credit customer (trade debtor) may fail to pay his/her debt. Under such a situation, the business carries an asset that is not going to be realised.

The prudence concept states that provision is made for all known liabilities (expenses or losses), whether the amount of these is known with certainty, or is a best estimate in the light of the information available.

With this in mind, there are two alternatives to choose from:

- write off the bad debt as irrecoverable;
- make a provision against a doubtful debt (specific provision).

In addition, businesses often make a general provision for doubtful debts.

Therefore, when a business realises that a trade debtor has defaulted, it makes sense to remove the debt from the books – write off the bad debt as irrecoverable – and recognise the loss that has been suffered. The *double entry* is: debit the bad debts expense account (an expense account in the profit and loss account), and credit the trade debtors (removing the debt from the books).

If the business receives, in subsequent years, an amount by the defaulted customer (who was treated as bad debt), then the business has managed to recover a debt previously written off. The *double entry* is: debit the bank or cash account, and credit the bad debt expense account.

Even if a customer has not yet defaulted, a business may have reasons to suspect that he/she will do so. And even in cases where there is no specific suspicion, past experience will indicate to a business that a certain proportion of its debts will never be collected and the likely level of possible defaulters. To cater for this situation, a provision (or an allowance) is made and businesses may open an account called 'provision for doubtful debts'.

Providing for a debt that is doubtful is different from writing off a debt that is definitely bad. A debt that is merely doubtful should not be written out of the trade debtors account; in other words, do not make the entry 'credit trade debtors'. The correct *double entry* when making or *increasing* a provision for doubtful debts is: debit the bad debts expense account, and credit the provision for doubtful debts account. Conversely, when the provision for doubtful debts is *decreasing*, the *double entry* is: debit the provision for doubtful debts account, and credit the bad debts expense account (i.e. opposite of the increasing provision).

The amount entered in the above two double entries is the *difference* in the provision for doubtful debts between the beginning of the year and the end of the year. The provision for doubtful debts at the end of the year represents the level of provision required by the business, and the adjustment to the existing level of the provision is done by using one of the above two double entries.

Consequently, the difference in the provision for doubtful debts between the beginning of the year and the end of the year appears in the profit and loss account as an expense (via the bad debts expense account). The eventual balance on the provision for doubtful debts account is shown as a deduction from trade debtors in the balance sheet.

Finally, when a business decides to write off a defaulted trade debtor as bad debt against which provision has already been made (maybe in a previous year), the correct *double entry* is: debit the provision for doubtful debts account, and credit the trade debtors account.

The use of both the bad debts expense account and the provision for doubtful debts account ensures that the trade debtors asset in the balance sheet is not over-valued.

Suspense accounts

A suspense account is a temporary 'holding' account onto which we place amounts in order to make the trial balance totals agree. Eventually, the business must establish the nature of the suspense balance and make the necessary entries to clear it.

Errors concerning relatively large ('material') amounts should be found before the profit and loss account and balance sheet are drawn up. If a discrepancy for a smaller amount cannot be explained, then we do not allow this to delay the preparation of the final accounts. Instead, a suspense account is drawn up.

There are two fairly common reasons why a suspense account could be opened:

- A bookkeeper is unsure where to post an item and enters it to a suspense account pending instructions. An example of this is when money is received by a business for a reason which is not immediately clear to the accountant. In such a case he/she would debit the amount to cash/bank, and would make the credit entry in a temporary suspense account. (Less commonly, the book-keeper might be unclear about the nature of a cash payment made by the business.)

- There is a difference in a trial balance, so that the total debits do not equal the total credits. As a result, a suspense account is opened with the amount of the difference so that the trial balance agrees (pending the discovery and correction of the errors causing the difference). This is the only time an entry is made in the records without a corresponding entry elsewhere.

Short questions

Question

Springsteen has paid rent of £1,200 for the period 1 January 2009 to 31 December 2009. His first accounts are prepared for the ten months ended 31 October 2009. What should his first accounts show?

Answer

His first accounts should show a rent expense of £1,000 in the profit and loss account, and a prepayment of £200 as a current asset in the balance sheet.

Question

At 1 January 2009 the accounts of a trader show accrued rent payable of £800. During the year she pays rent bills totalling £9,000, including one bill for £450 in respect of the quarter ending 31 January 2010. What is the profit and loss charge for rent for the year ended 31 December 2009?

Answer

There is a prepayment of £150 (1/3 × £450) on 31 December 2009, so the profit and loss account charge for the rent expense is £8,050.

The T-account would look like this:

Rent expense

2009			2009		
31 Dec.	Bank	9,000	1 Jan.	Balance b/d	800
				P&L a/c	8,050
				Balance c/d	150
		9,000			9,000

Question

A company has made the following payments in respect of electricity and internet expenses:

	Date paid	Amount £
Electricity		
Quarter ended 31 Jan. 2007	02.01.2007	450
Quarter ended 30 Apr. 2007	28.01.2007	450
Quarter ended 31 July 2007	31.04.2007	630
Quarter ended 31 Oct. 2007	30.07.2007	630
Quarter ended 31 Jan. 2008	01.11.2007	630

	Date paid	Amount £
Internet		
Quarter ended 30 Nov. 2006	01.02.2007	525
Quarter ended 28 Feb. 2007	01.04.2007	495
Quarter ended 31 May 2007	17.07.2007	600
Quarter ended 31 Aug. 2007	12.10.2007	570
Quarter ended 30 Nov. 2007	01.02.2008	720
Quarter ended 28 Feb. 2008	02.04.2008	660

The company has a calendar year end.

1 What balance should have been brought down in the electricity expense account at 1 January 2007?

2 What balance should have been brought down in the internet expense account at 1 January 2007?

3 What balance should be carried down in the electricity expense account at 31 December 2007?

4 What balance should be carried down in the internet expense account at 31 December 2007?

5 What is the charge for electricity in the profit and loss account for the year ended 31 December 2007?

6 What is the charge for internet in the profit and loss account for the year ended 31 December 2007?

Answer

1 The company should have accrued an amount in respect of the months of November and December 2006, i.e. $2/3 \times £450 = £300$ balance brought down (on the credit side).

2 The company should have accrued an amount in respect of the month of December 2006, i.e. $1/3 \times £495 = £165$, but the company also owed the

quarter ended 30 November 2006 at the end of the accounting period (since it was paid on 1 February 2007), and as a result the accrued amount brought down was (£165 + 525) £690 balance brought down (on the credit side).

3 The bill for the quarter ended 31 January 2008 was paid on 1 November 2007, but only two-thirds of this bill (i.e. November and December 2007) were related to 2008. Hence, the balance is a prepayment at 31 December 2007, that is 1/3 × £630 = £210 balance carried down (on the credit side).

4 The company should have accrued one-third of the bill for the quarter ended 28 February 2008, i.e. the amount for the month December 2007 was not paid by the end of the year, hence the amount is 1/3 × £660 = £220. However, the company also owed the quarter ended 30 November 2007 at the end of the accounting period (since it was paid on 1 February 2008), and as a result the accrued amount carried down was (£220 + 720) £940 balance carried down (on the debit side).

5 It should be £150 + 450 + 630 + 630 + 420 = £2,280. The T-account should look like this:

Electricity expense

2007			2007		
31 Dec.	Bank	2,790	1 Jan.	Balance b/d	300
			31 Dec.	P&L a/c	2,280
				Balance c/d	210
		2,790			2,790

6 It should be £330 + 600 + 570 + 720 + 220 = £2,440. The T-account should look like this:

Internet expense

2007			2007		
31 Dec.	Bank	2,190	1 Jan.	Balance b/d	690
	Balance c/d	940		P&L a/c	2,440
		3,130			3,130

Question

A rent accrual of £450 was treated as a prepayment in preparing the profit and loss account of a business. What is the effect on the profit of the year?

Answer

We know that, as a rule of thumb, the accruals at the end of the year are added to the relevant expense accounts, while the prepayments at the end of the year are deducted from the relevant expense accounts. With this in mind, and by classing a liability as an asset, the business has improved the profit figure. In effect, the business has treated the amount as a £450 increase in profit, instead of a £450 deduction from profit. The net effect is to overstate profit by £900.

Question

An electricity accrual of £400 was ignored completely when preparing a trader's profit and loss account. What is the result of the above?

Answer

Profit was overstated by £400 in the profit and loss account, and current liabilities understated by £400 in the balance sheet.

We know that, as a rule of thumb, the accruals at the end of the year are added to the relevant expense accounts. With this in mind, and by ignoring a liability at the end of the year, the business has improved the profit figure, and reduced the amount of liabilities.

Question

Costa's business had debtors of £100 at 1 February 2007 and £90 at 31 January 2008. Credit sales amounted to £790 and cash received from debtors was £770; a bad debt of £10 was written off. How much discount was allowed to customers during the year?

Answer

The discount allowed was £20. The T-account should look like this:

Trade debtors

1 Feb.	Balance b/d	100		Bank	770
	Sales	790		Bad debt	10
				Disc. allowed	20
			31 Jan.	Balance c/d	90
		890			890

Question

On 1 January 2008 Scottish Castle Ltd had a balance on its debtors account and a provision for doubtful debts as follows:

Dr balance   £1,840,000
Cr balance   £9,200

On 31 December 2008 the balance on the debtors account was £1,600,000. The company's management then decided to write off balances of £30,000 as bad debts and to make a provision of 0.5 percent against the remaining total debtors.

What would be the totals which appear in the profit and loss account and balance sheet following the above adjustments?

Answer

There will be total charges of £28,650 in the profit and loss account, and the trade debtors figure would be £1,562,150 in the balance sheet.

The calculations are as follows: The remaining debtors after bad debts at the end of the year are £1,570,000 (£1,600,000 − 30,000). Hence, the provision for doubtful debts at the end of the year is going to be £7,850 (£1,570,000 × 0.5%). There is a decrease in the provision for doubtful debts of £1,350, which is a credit entry in the bad debts expense account. Therefore, overall, the bad debts expense account has already got a debit entry of £30,000, and the net effect is a charge of £28,650 in the profit and loss account.

Similarly, the provision for doubtful debts at the end of the year is deductable from the remaining debtors, which comes to £1,562,150 in the balance sheet (£1,600,000 − 30,000 − 7,850).

Question

A business starts its year with £800 in the provision for doubtful debts account. At the end of the year, debtors total £12,000 of which £600 are considered doubtful. What is the effect on the profit and loss account and balance sheet?

Answer

£200 is added to profit and the balance sheet shows trade debtors less provision as £11,400.

Question

A business had a suspense account balance of £580 (debit) before the following errors were detected and corrected:

a £140 worth of credit sales had been entered on the sales account but not on the debtors account.

b A payment of £165 to a creditor had been entered in their account, but the cash book had not received any entry for this transaction.

What should the double-entries be for correcting these errors?

Answer

Debit debtor £140, credit suspense £140; and credit bank £165, debit suspense £165.

The debtors account needs an entry to reflect the increase in debt. This can only be achieved by debiting that account. The bank account should have had a payment recorded from it. This can only be achieved by crediting that account. In each case, the suspense account receives the other half of the double entry.

Question

Referring back to the information in the previous question, what would the revised balance on the suspense account be?

Answer

£605 (debit)

£580 (debit) is the opening balance. The account will receive a credit of £140, reducing the balance to £440 debit, but then a further debit of £165 will increase the balance to £605 debit.

Questions

Question 1

A business has an accounting year ending on 31 December. At 31 December 2007 the records contained the following accounts:

	£
Trade debtors	19,000
Provision for bad debts	1,000

The trade debtors at 31 December 2008 were £18,900. The business decided at the end of the year to write off balances of £300 as bad debts. The trade debtors figure includes amounts of £250 owed by business C, £150 owed by business M, and £200 owed by business A, all of which are regarded as doubtful debts.

Required

What is going to be the provision for doubtful debts as at 31 December 2008, given a general provision of 5 percent of trade debtors was applied? Show the T-accounts entries in respect of the above and the relevant profit and loss account and balance sheet extracts. Use the blank T-accounts provided below.

Bad debts expense

Provision for doubtful debts

Question 2

This is a continuation of the above question.

During the year ended 31 December 2009, business C was declared bankrupt and a first payment of £150 was received by the administrator (this payment was not the final payment). Business M was also declared bankrupt and a first and final payment of £30 was received by the administrator. Business A paid its debt in full during the year. A further debt of £350 owed by business R that is included in the debtors at 31 December 2009 proved to be bad.

The trade debtors at 31 December 2009 were £22,070. This figure is the final figure of trade debtors before taking into account bad debts.

Required

What is going to be the provision for doubtful debts as at 31 December 2009, given a general provision of 5 percent of trade debtors was applied? Show the T-accounts entries in respect of the above and the relevant profit and loss account and balance sheet extracts. Use the blank T-accounts provided below.

Business C

Business M

Business R

Bad debts expense

Provision for doubtful debts

Question 3

A business's provision for doubtful debts was £900 on 31 December 2005. During the year ended 31 December 2006, the business received £200 from a trade debtor towards the settlement of a debt of £565 which had been written off as bad debt by the business in 2001. This payment of £200 seems to be the final payment of that trade debtor to the business.

Trade debtors at 31 December 2006 amounted to £20,400, and bad debts decided to be written off at the end of the year are as follows: Business A £950 and Business X £450.

The provision for doubtful debts continues to be 5 percent of debtors at the year-end.

Required
Show the T-accounts entries in respect of the above and the relevant profit and loss account and balance sheet extracts.

Question 4

At the end of the calendar year 2007, the provision for doubtful debts account is 2.5 percent of the trade debtors of £40,000 on that date. During the year 2008, bad debts of £2,500 were written off. At the end of calendar year 2008, the provision for doubtful debts is required to be 2.5 percent against debtors of £48,000.

In the year 2009, bad debts of £100 are to be written off. At the end of calendar year 2009, a provision of 0.8 percent against debtors of £87,500 is required.

Required
Record the above transactions using T-accounts.

Question 5

The trade debtors account as at 31 December 2004 was £39,800. The provision for doubtful debts at the same date was 3.5 percent of the balance outstanding from debtors.

During 2005, the company's sales totalled £350,000, of which 91 percent, in value, was on credit and £318,150 was received from credit customers in settlement of their debts totalling £320,000. In addition, £450 was received from a trade debtor in a settlement of a debt which had been written off as bad during 2004.

On 31 December 2005, the following outstanding debts were written off as bad: Business F £280 and Business H £920.

The provision for doubtful debts continues to be 3.5 percent of debtors at the year-end.

Required
1 Show the double-entry for the trade debtors, bad debts and the provision for doubtful debts accounts for the year ended 31 December 2006.

2 Show the relevant balance sheet extract.

Question 6

Your local newsagent has an accounting year ending on 31 December. The following amounts have been paid for gas heating:

Date paid	Quarter ended	£
20 March 2004	29 February 2004	105
28 June 2004	31 May 2004	74
30 September 2004	31 August 2004	79
5 January 2005	30 November 2004	89
25 March 2005	28 February 2005	114

Required

You are required to show the double entries in the light and heat account for the year ended 31 December 2004 and the relevant balance sheet extract. Use the blank T-account provided below.

Light and heat

Question 7

Your local fish 'n' chips has an accounting year ending on 31 December. The following amounts have been paid as electricity:

Date paid	Quarter ended	£
2 December 2007	28 February 2007	900
1 March 2007	31 May 2007	930
4 June 2007	31 August 2008	960
5 September 208	30 November 2008	990
4 December 2008	28 February 2008	1,020

Required

You are required to show the double-entries in the light and heat account for the year ended 31 December 2007 and the relevant balance sheet extract. Use the blank T-account provided below.

Light and heat

Question 8

Your local internet café has an accounting year ending on 31 December. The following amounts have been paid in respect of telephone and internet:

Expense	Date paid	Quarter ended	£
Telephone	02.11.07	31.01.08	750
Telephone	01.02.08	30.04.08	780
Telephone	01.05.08	31.07.08	795
Telephone	01.08.08	31.10.08	795
Telephone	03.11.08	31.01.09	825
Internet	03.03.08	28.02.08	840
Internet	02.06.08	31.05.08	825
Internet	01.09.08	31.08.08	855
Internet	01.12.08	30.11.08	870
Internet	02.03.09	28.02.09	885

Required

You are required to show the double-entries in the telephone account and internet account (create two separate accounts) for the year ended 31 December 2008.

Question 9

A supermarket's financial year runs from 1 January to 31 December and the business maintains a combined rent and rates account. Rent is payable quarterly in advance. Rent was £4,200 for the 12-month period ended 31 July 2008 and is £4,440 for the 12-month period ending 31 July 2009.

The following amounts have been paid in respect of rent:

Date paid	Quarter ended	£
02.08.07	31.10.07	1,050
01.11.07	31.01.08	1,050
01.02.08	30.04.08	1,050
01.05.08	31.07.08	1,050
03.08.08	31.10.08	1,110
02.11.08	31.01.09	1,110

Rates are assessed annually for the year from 1 November to the following 31 October and are payable in one lump sum by 30 April. The rates assessment was £2,400 for the year ended 31 October 2008 (which was paid on 30 April 2008) and £2,700 for the year ended 31 October 2009 (which was paid on 30 April 2009).

Required
You are required to show the double-entries in the rent and rates account for the year ended 31 December 2008.

Question 10

You are given the balances of the following accounts as at 1 July 2007:

	£
Vehicles (at cost)	14,850
Provision for depreciation of vehicles	7,510
Rent and rates – accrued	3,100
– prepaid	2,890

During the financial year of the business, the following transactions took place:

Traded-in vehicle – original cost	5,320
– accumulated depreciation	3,690
– part-exchange allowance	1,750
Paid balance of price of new vehicle by cheque	9,200
Paid rent by cheque	6,140
Paid rates by cheque	4,120

Closing balances as at 30 June 2008 were:

Vehicles (at cost)	To be derived
Provision for depreciation of vehicles	4,430
Rent and rates – accrued	2,990
– prepaid	2,440

Required
You are required to show the double entries for all the accounts above for the year ended 30 June 2008.

Answers

Question 1

Requirement 1

Calculation of provision for doubtful debts at 31 December 2008:

	£
Specific provision – business C	250
– business M	150
– business A	200
Total specific provision	600
General provision – (£18,900 – £300 – £600) × 5%	900
Specific plus general provision	1,500

Bad debts expense

2008		£	2008		£
31 Dec.	Bad debts	300			
	Provision	500	31 Dec.	Profit and loss a/c	800
		800			800

Provision for doubtful debts

2008		£	2008		£
31 Dec.	Balance c/d	1,500	1 Jan.	Balance b/d	1,000
			31 Dec.	Bad debts expense	500
		1,500			1,500
2009					
			1 Jan.	Balance b/d	1,500

Profit and loss account	£
Bad debts	300
Provision for doubtful debts	500

Balance sheet	£
Current assets	
Debtors (18,900 – 300)	18,600
Less Provision for doubtful debts	1,500
	17,100

Question 2

Requirement 1

Calculation of provision for doubtful debts at 31 December 2009:

	£
Specific provision – business C (£250 – £150)	100
General provision – (£22,070 – £120 – £350 – £100) × 5%	1,075
Specific plus general provision	1,175

Business C

2009		£	2009		£
1 Jan.	Balance b/d	250	31 Dec.	Bank	150
			31 Dec.	Balance c/d	100
		250			250
2010					
1 Jan.	Balance b/d	100			

Business M

2009		£	2009		£
1 Jan.	Balance b/d	150	31 Dec.	Bank	30
			31 Dec.	Bad debts	120
		150			150

Business R

2009		£	2009		£
1 Jan.	Balance b/d	350	31 Dec.	Bad debts	350

Bad debts expense

2009		£	2009		£
31 Dec.	Business M	120	31 Dec.	Provision	325
31 Dec.	Business R	350	31 Dec.	Profit and loss a/c	145
		470			470

Provision for doubtful debts

2009		£	2009		£
31 Dec.	Bad debts expense	325	1 Jan.	Balance b/d	1,500
31 Dec.	Balance c/d	1,175			
		1,500			1,500
			2010		
			1 Jan.	Balance b/d	1,175

Profit and loss account	£
Bad debts	470
Provision for doubtful debts	(325)

Balance sheet	£
Current assets	
Debtors (£22,070 − £120 − £350)	21,600
Less Provision for doubtful debts	1,175
	20,425

Question 3

Requirement 1
Calculation of provision for doubtful debts at 31 December 2006:

$$5\% \times (£20,400 - £1,400) = £950$$

Bad debts expense

2006		£	2006		£
31 Dec.	Business A	950	31 Dec.	Bank	200
31 Dec.	Business X	450	31 Dec.	P/L a/c	1,250
	Provision	50			
		1,450			1,450

Provision for bad debts

2006		£	2006		£
			1 Jan.	Balance b/d	900
31 Dec.	Balance c/d	950	31 Dec.	Bad debts expense	50
		950			950
			2007		
			1 Jan.	Balance b/d	950

Profit and loss account	£
Bad debts	1,200
Provision for doubtful debts	50

Balance sheet	
Current assets	£
Debtors (£20,400 – £1,400)	19,000
Less Provision for doubtful debts	950
	18,050

Question 4

Requirement 1

Bad debts expense

2008		£	2008		£
During	Trade debtors	2,500			
31 Dec.	Provision	200	31 Dec.	Profit and loss a/c	2,700
		2,700			2,700

Provision for bad debts

2008		£	2008		£
			1 Jan.	Balance b/d	1,000
31 Dec.	Balance c/d	1,200	31 Dec.	Bad debts expense	200
		1,200			1,200
			2009		
			1 Jan.	Balance b/d	1,200

Bad debts expense

2009		£	2009		£
During	Trade debtors	100	31 Dec.	Provision	500
31 Dec.	Profit and loss a/c	400			
		500			500

Provision for bad debts

2009		£	2009		£
31 Dec.	Bad debts expense	500	1 Jan.	Balance b/d	1,200
31 Dec.	Balance c/d	700			
		1,200			1,200
			2010		
			1 Jan.	Balance b/d	700

Question 5

Requirement 1

Trade debtors

2005	£	2005	£
Balance b/d	39,800	Bank	318,150
Sales		Discount allowed	
(91% × 350,000)	318,500	(320,000 − 318,150)	1,850
		Bad debts	1,200
		Balance c/d	37,100
	358,300		358,300

Calculation of provision for doubtful debts at 31 December 2004:

3.5% × £39,800 = £1,393

Calculation of provision for doubtful debts at 31 December 2005:

3.5% × £37,100 = £1,299

Bad debts expense

2005		£	2005		£
31 Dec.	Trade debtors	1,200	31 Dec.	Bank	450
			31 Dec.	Provision	94
			31 Dec.	Profit and loss a/c	656
		1,200			1,200

Provision for bad debts

2005		£	2005		£
31 Dec.	Bad debts expense	94	1 Jan.	Balance b/d	1,393
	Balance c/d	1,299			
		1,393			1,393
			2007		
			1 Jan.	Balance b/d	1,299

Requirement 2

Balance sheet	£
Current assets	
Debtors	37,100
Less Provision for doubtful debts	1,299
	35,801

Question 6

Requirement 1

Accrual at 1 January 2004:

$1/3 \times £105 = £35$

Accrual at 31 December 2004:

$£89 + (1/3 \times £114) = £127$

Light and heat

2004		£	2004		£
20 Mar.	Bank	105	1 Jan.	Accrual b/d	35
28 June	Bank	74	31 Dec.	Profit and loss a/c	350
30 Sept.	Bank	79			
31 Dec.	Accrual c/d	127			
		385			385
			2005		
			1 Jan.	Accrual b/d	127

Balance sheet as at 31 December 2004

	£
Current liabilities	
Accrued expenses	127

Question 7

Requirement 1

Prepaid at 1 January 2007:

$2/3 \times £900 = £600$

Prepaid at 31 December 2007:

$2/3 \times £1,020 = £680$

Light and heat

2007		£	2007		£
1 Jan.	Prepayment b/d	600	31 Dec.	Profit and loss a/c	3,820
1 Mar.	Bank	930			
4 June	Bank	960	31 Dec.	Prepayment c/d	680
5 Sept.	Bank	990			
4 Dec.	Bank	1,020			
		4,500			4,500
2008					
1 Jan.	Prepayment b/d	680			

Balance sheet as at 31 December 2007

	£
Current assets	
Prepaid expenses	680

Question 8

Requirement 1

Telephone prepaid on 1 January 2008:

$1/3 \times £750 = £250$ [one month has been paid last year]

Telephone prepaid on 31 December 2008:

$1/3 \times £825 = £275$ [one month prepayment for next year]

Internet accrued on 1 January 2008:

$1/3 \times £840 = £280$ [one month owed from last year]

Internet accrued on 31 December 2008:

$1/3 \times £885 = £295$ [one month is owed at the end of year]

Telephone

2008		£	2008		£
1 Jan.	Prepayment b/d	250			
1 Feb.	Bank	780	31 Dec.	Profit and loss a/c	3,170
1 May	Bank	795			
1 Aug.	Bank	795	31 Dec.	Prepayment c/d	275
3 Nov.	Bank	825			
		3,445			3,445
2009					
1 Jan.	Prepayment b/d	275			

Internet

2008		£	2008		£
3 Mar.	Bank	840	1 Jan.	Accrual b/d	280
2 June	Bank	825	31 Dec.	Profit and loss a/c	3,405
1 Sept.	Bank	855			
1 Dec.	Bank	870			
31 Dec.	Accrual c/d	295			
		3,685			3,685
			2009		
			1 Jan.	Accrual b/d	295

Question 9

Requirement 1

Rent prepaid at 1 January 2008:	$1/3 \times £1,050 = £350$
Rent prepaid at 31 December 2008:	$1/3 \times £1,110 = £370$
Rates accrued at 1 January 2008:	$2/12 \times £2,400 = £400$
Rates accrued at 31 December 2008:	$2/12 \times £2,700 = £450$

Rent and rates

2008		£	2008		£
1 Jan.	Prepayment b/d	350	1 Jan.	Accrual b/d	400
1 Feb.	Bank	1,050	31 Dec.	Profit and loss a/c	6,750
30 Apr.	Bank	2,400			
1 May	Bank	1,050	31 Dec.	Prepayment c/d	370
3 Aug.	Bank	1,110			
2 Nov.	Bank	1,110			
31 Dec.	Accrual c/d	450			
		7,520			7,520
2009			2009		
1 Jan.	Prepayment b/d	370	1 Jan.	Accrual b/d	450

Question 10

Requirement 1

Profit on sale of vehicle: $(£5,320 - £3,690) - £1,750 = \underline{£120}$

Rent and rates

2007		£	2007		£
1 July	Prepayment b/d	2,890	1 July	Accrual b/d	3,100
2008			2008		
30 June	Bank	6,140	30 June	Profit and loss a/c	10,600
30 June	Bank	4,120			
30 June	Accrual c/d	2,990	30 June	Prepayment c/d	2,440
		16,140			16,140
2008			2008		
1 July	Prepayment b/d	2,440	1 July	Accrual b/d	2,990

Vehicles – cost

2007		£	2007		£
1 July	Balance b/d	14,850			
2008			2008		
30 June	Bank	9,200	30 June	Disposal	5,320
30 June	Part exchange	1,750	30 June	Balance c/d	20,480
		25,800			25,800
1 July	Balance b/d	20,480			

Vehicles – provision for depreciation

2007		£	2007		£
1 July	Disposal	3,690	1 July	Balance b/d	7,510
2008			2008		
30 June	Balance c/d	4,430	30 June	Depreciation expense	610
		8,120			8,120
			1 July	Balance b/d	4,430

Vehicles – Depreciation expense

2008		£	2008		£
30 June	Provision for depreciation	610	30 June	Profit and loss a/c	610

Vehicles – disposal

2008		£	2008		£
30 June	Vehicles – cost	5,320	30 June	Provision for depreciation	3,690
30 June	Profit on disposal	120		Proceeds (part exchange)	1,750
		5,440			5,440

Chapter 6

Incomplete records

This chapter covers briefly the following topics:

- Forms of incomplete records
- Ways of dealing with incomplete records
- Sales and trade debtors, purchases and trade creditors
- Gross margin and mark-up
- Incomplete information with regards to cash

Forms of incomplete records

Many businesses (especially small) do not keep a full set of accounting records. Even where full records are maintained, there is a danger that they may be accidentally lost or destroyed.

The general term 'incomplete records' refers to the situation where the transactions of a business have not been recorded in double-entry form.

There are three forms of incomplete records:

1 *Incomplete records of income and expenditure*
There are no basic documents or records of revenue income and expenditure, or the records are inadequate.

This situation arises:

- when accounting books and documents have been accidentally destroyed (e.g. in a fire or floods), and/or
- all necessary and relevant information is available but bookkeeping is incomplete (e.g. the owner has failed to keep proper accounting records).

2 *Complete 'single entry'*
All business transactions have been entered in a book of prime entry, usually a cash book, and not in the general ledger. In other words, all necessary and relevant information is available but bookkeeping is incomplete.

3 Incomplete 'single entry'
This is a variation on point 2 above: there are no books of account (or these are incomplete), but the *receipts* and *payments* can be ascertained from the *bank statements* and/or supporting documents.

Ways of dealing with incomplete records

The question posed here is how do we cope with the problems of incomplete records and ultimately prepare final accounts. Well, let's take each form of incomplete record separately and try to provide some answers.

1 Dealing with incomplete records of income and expenditure
When this form of incomplete records arises, then it is obvious that a profit and loss account cannot be prepared.

However, providing necessary and relevant information is available relating to assets and liabilities *at the start* **and** *end* of the accounting period, then the profit (or loss) for the year can be calculated by comparing the two balance sheets.

In other words, we use the *'changes in the owners' equity'* formula that we have seen in Chapter 1 to derive the profit (or loss) for the period:

$$OE = OC + P \ (or - L) + NC - D$$

where:
   OE = owner's equity or closing capital;
   OC = opening capital;
    P = profits;
    L = losses;
   NC = new capital introduced by the owners;
    D = drawings.

We can re-arrange the above equation to provide a formula for calculating the profit (P) or loss (L) made by a business during an accounting period.

2 Dealing with complete 'single entry'
When this form of incomplete records arises, then simply the bookkeeping is completed by posting the transactions to the nominal ledger, i.e. the double entry is completed. The financial statements then can be prepared.

3 Dealing with incomplete 'single entry'
This is possibly the most difficult to 'deal with' form of incomplete records and involves the following steps:

- produce a cash book summary from the information given on the bank statements;

- calculate missing information for income or expenses as *balancing figures* on assets and liability accounts

    for example: credit sales as balancing figure on trade debtors a/c, credit purchases as balancing figure on trade creditors a/c (see also below the relevant section);

- make estimates (if necessary)

    for example: sales from cost of goods sold (COGS) using gross profit %, or mark-up cost % (see also below the relevant section).

After having done any or all of the above, the financial statements can be prepared.

Sales and trade debtors, purchases and trade creditors

Sales and trade debtors

The basic trade debtors account links:

- sales, cash receipts and debtors.

If the credit sales information for the period is missing, then we 'force out' those sales as a balancing figure from the trade debtors account, using the following *basic* T-account formula:

Opening debtors + Sales – Cash receipts = Closing debtors

Note: the above is the *basic* trade debtors T-account, and other items may need to be included (for example, bad debts, discounts given, etc.).

Also note that any cash sales can be ascertained from the bank statements and/or supporting documents.

Purchases and trade creditors

The basic trade creditors account links:

- purchases, cash payments and creditors.

If the credit purchases information for the period is missing, then we 'force out' those purchases as a balancing figure from the trade creditors account, using the following *basic* T-account formula:

Opening creditors + Purchases – Cash payments = Closing creditors

Note: the above is the *basic* trade creditors T-account, and other items may need to be included (for example, discounts received, etc.).

Also note that any cash purchases can be ascertained from the bank statements and/or supporting documents.

The above calculations to arrive at the figures for sales and purchases can take place providing there is a record of *closing* trade debtors and trade creditors.

Opening trade debtors and trade creditors are known from last year's balance sheet, and cash movements are determined from the bank statements.

Gross margin and mark-up

Some problems with incomplete records concern the relationship between sales, cost of goods sold and gross profit. To help us better understand this relationship, let's look at an example:

	%
Sales	125
(−) COGS	100
Gross profit (GP)	25

As gross profit (GP) may be expressed *either* as a percentage of the cost of goods sold (COGS) *or* as a percentage of sales, then in the example above:

- gross profit is 25 percent of cost of goods sold (i.e. 25/100). The terminology is a *25 percent mark-up* (*cost*);

- gross profit can also be expressed as 20 percent of sales (i.e. 25/125). The terminology is a *20 percent gross profit margin* or *20 percent gross profit percentage*.

We may also need to use the above concepts to calculate an unknown figure. For example, the number of sales or the cost of goods sold may need to be calculated.

The *mark-up formula* is as follows:

Mark-up cost % = GP/COGS

By working out the above equation, we get:

→ Sales/COGS = 1 + Mark-up cost %

We then solve for the unknown:

- if Sales, then

   Sales = COGS × (1 + Mark-up cost %)

- if COGS, then

   COGS = Sales/(1 + Mark-up cost %)

The *gross profit margin formula* is as follows:

GP margin % = GP/Sales

By working out the above equation, we get:

→ COGS/sales = 1 − GP margin % →

We then solve for the unknown:

- if Sales, then

    Sales = COGS/(1 – GP margin %)

- if COGS, then

    COGS = Sales × (1 – GP margin %)

The above formulas may also help us to calculate the unknown figure for stock. The procedure here is usually to work out the cost of goods sold using the gross profit margin or mark-up equations given above, and then to use the formula which we saw in Chapter 3:

    Opening stock + Purchases – Closing stock = Cost of goods sold

The value of the missing stock can then be calculated as a balancing figure in the above equation.

Incomplete information with regards to cash

Some problems with incomplete records revolve around missing information when a business owner sells mainly for cash.

The main problem may arise when business's expenses or private drawings (by the owner) may be paid out of cash without being recorded in the books of the business.

Hence, there will be a missing *credit* in the cash account (not balance).[1]

The business owner is breaking the rule that *all* takings should be *banked* intact[2] and that *cash* should be drawn *out of the bank to pay expenses and drawings*.

The procedure in this case is as follows:

- keep *separate* accounts for bank and cash needed;
- enter in the credit of the cash account all amounts known to have been paid from till receipts, such as expenses, drawings and lodgements into bank;
- then enter in the debit of the cash account all receipts from cash customers or other sources;

---

1 *Note*: the bank account records cheques drawn on the business bank account and cheques received from customers and other sources. The cash account records till receipts and any expenses or drawings paid out of till receipts *before* banking.
2 When cash receipts are lodged in the bank, then debit the bank account and credit the cash account.

- Finally, calculate whether a debit or credit entry is required in order for the cash account to balance and force out the missing debit or credit as a *balancing figure* in that account:
  - if the balancing figure is a large debit, then this will represent the value of cash sales (if that is the unknown figure);
  - if the balancing figure is a credit entry, then this will represent the amount of cash drawings or of cash stolen.

Short questions

Question

The following information is available in respect of a sole trader:

	€
Drawings	9,500
Net profit for the year	8,000
Capital at the end of the year	25,000

No new capital was introduced by the owner during the year.

What is the business's opening capital?

Answer

Using the '*changes in the owners' equity*' formula, we can derive the opening capital for the period:

$$OE = OC + P + NC - D$$
$$\therefore \quad OC = OE - P - NC + D = 25,000 - 8,000 - 0 + 9,500 = 26,500$$

Therefore, the net assets of the business (i.e. the owner's equity) have fallen over the year by £1,500.

Question

Madge does not keep full accounting records, but the following information is available in respect of her accounting year ended 31 March 2009:

	£
Trade creditors at 1 April 2008	22,870
Trade creditors at 31 March 2009	19,530
Cash purchases during the year	52,248
Cash paid for goods supplied on credit	81,549

In her profit and loss account for the year ended 31 March 2009, what will be Madge's figure for purchases?

Answer

We can calculate the missing information with regards to credit purchases as a *balancing figure* on the trade creditors account.

In other words, using the trade creditors T-account:

Trade creditors

	£	£	
Bank	81,549	22,870	Bal b/d
Bal c/d	19,530	78,209	*Purchases*
			(balancing figure)
	101,079	101,079	

Or the following formula:

Opening creditors + Purchases − Cash payments = Closing creditors

we get:

Credit purchases = Closing creditors − Opening creditors + Cash payments
= 19,530 − 22,870 + 81,549 = £78,209

Therefore, Madge's total purchases amount to cash purchases *plus* credit purchases £(52,248 + 78,209) = £130,457.

Question
The following information is available:

	£
Sales	300,000
Opening stock	25,000
Purchases	250,000
Closing stock	30,000

Calculate: (a) the mark-up (cost), and (b) the gross profit margin.

Answer
a The cost of goods sold (COGS) is £245,000 and gross profit (GP) is therefore £55,000. The mark-up cost is:

GP/COGS = (£55,000/£245,000) × 100% = 22.45%

b The GP margin is:

GP/sales = (£55,000/£300,000) × 100% = $18^{1}/_{3}\%$

Question
If sales are £20,000 and the gross profit margin is 20 percent, what is the cost of goods sold?

Answer
We solve the GP margin formula for the unknown gross profit, as follows:

$$GP = GP \text{ margin} \times Sales = 20\% \times £20,000 = £4,000$$
$$\therefore \quad \text{Cost of goods sold} = Sales - GP = £(20,000 - 4,000) = £16,000$$

Question

Fergie is a sole trader. The following information is available in respect of her accounting year ended 31 March 2009:

	Opening balance	Closing balance
	€	€
Stock	5,000	1,500
Trade creditors	2,500	4,800
Trade debtors	4,000	5,500

Fergie's bank statements for the year show receipts from trade debtors of €80,000 and payments to trade creditors of €55,000.

What is Fergie's gross profit margin?

Answer

We can calculate the missing information with regards to *purchases* as a *balancing figure* on the trade creditors account.

In other words, using the trade creditors T-account:

Trade creditors

	€	€	
Bank	55,000	2,500	Bal b/d
Bal c/d	4,800	57,300	*Purchases*
			(balancing figure)
	59,800	59,800	

We can calculate the missing information with regards to *sales* as a *balancing figure* on the trade debtors account.

In other words, using the trade debtors T-account:

Trade debtors

	€	€	
Bal b/d	4,000	80,000	Bank
Sales	81,500	5,500	Bal c/d
(balancing figure)			
	85,500	85,500	

$$COGS = \text{Opening stock} + \text{Purchases} - \text{Closing stock}$$
$$= €(5,000 + 57,300 - 1,500) = €60,800$$

Therefore, the gross profit is going to be:

Sales − COGS = 81,500 − 60,800 = €20,700

and the gross profit margin is:

= €20,700/€81,500
= 25.39%

Question
Dixie's business achieves a gross profit margin of 40 percent and her cost of goods sold in 2009 was £480,000. All sales are for cash, and her cash account balance at the start and end of the accounting year were £10,000 and £8,000 respectively. Cash banked during the year amounted to £610,000 and cash expenses paid directly from the cash account were £22,000. Dixie cannot remember the amount of her own cash drawings and asks for your help.

Answer
Solving the GP margin formula, we get

Sales = COGS/(1 − GP margin %) = £480,000/0.60 = £800,000

Then, we can calculate the missing information with regards to *cash drawings* as a *balancing figure* on the cash account:

Cash account

	£	£	
Bal b/d	10,000	22,000	Expenses
Sales	800,000	610,000	Bank
		170,000	*Drawings (balancing figure)*
		8,000	Bal c/d
	810,000	810,000	

Question
Your local newsagent makes sales of £52,000 and purchases of £31,000 over the last accounting year. The owner took goods costing £455 without paying for them. Closing stock was valued at its cost of £1,200 and the gross profit margin achieved is 40 percent on sales.
   What is the cost of the opening stock?

Answer
We solve the GP margin formula for the unknown gross profit, as follows:

GP = GP margin × Sales = 40% × £52,000 = £20,800

It follows that COGS = (Sales − GP) = £(52,000 − 20,800) = £31,200.

Hence, using the COGS formula, we can derive the missing opening stock figure, as follows:

COGS = Opening stock + Purchases − Closing stock
∴ Opening stock = COGS − Purchases + Closing stock
        = £(31,200 − (31,000 − 455) + 1,200) = £1,855

Question

Harrison Ford has opening stock of €30,000 and makes purchases during the year of €340,000. He removes goods costing €1,500 for his own use, and the business achieves a constant mark-up of 20 percent on cost. Sales for the period are €360,000.

What is Harrison's closing stock?

Answer

Using the mark-up cost formula (GP/COGS) and replacing COGS with (Sales − GP), we get:

COGS = 5/6 × Sales = 5/6 × €360,000 = €300,000

Hence, using the COGS formula, we can derive the missing closing stock figure, as follows:

COGS = Opening stock + Purchases − Closing stock
∴ Closing stock = Opening stock + Purchases − COGS
        = €(30,000 + (340,000 − 1,500) − 300,000) = €68,500

Questions

Question 1

The trial balance of a business called 'Saturdays', a sole trader, at 1 January 2007 is as follows:

	Debit £000	Credit £000
Stock	300	
Trade debtors	480	
Trade creditors		150
Repayments – telephone and internet	34	
– advertising	16	
Accruals – accountant's fee		12
– rent and rates		3
Fixed assets	500	
Fixed assets – provision for depreciation		150
Capital		1,000
Bank		15
	1,330	1,330

During the financial year, the following transactions took place:

	£000
Owners' personal withdrawals	80
Depreciation	50
Receipts from customers	1,200
Bad debts written off	6
Payments to suppliers	900
Discounts allowed	10
Payments for – telephone and internet	90
– advertising	30
– accountant's fee	25
– rent and rates	13
– public relations service fee	250

At 31 December 2007 the closing account balances are as follows:

	£000
Stock	350
Trade debtors	250
Prepayments – telephone and internet	40
– rent and rates	5
Trade creditors	190
Accruals – accountant's fee	20
– advertising	10

Required

1 You are required to show the double-entries for the following accounts for the year ended 31 December 2007: bank, trade creditors, trade debtors, telephone and internet, advertising, accountant's fee, and rent and rates.

2 Prepare Saturdays' profit and loss account for the year.

3 Prepare Saturdays' balance sheet as at 31 December 2007.

Question 2

The owner of Bodystore, a retailer, does not keep proper books of accounts, but was able to supply his accountant with the following information on 1 April 2008:

	£
Fixtures and fittings	5,500
Freehold premises	85,000
Trade debtors	5,700
Bank	19,854
Cash	100
Stock	25,000
Trade creditors	7,440

The following is a summary of his *bank* statement for the year ended 31 March 2009:

	£
Takings banked	41,200
Interest from private investment received	1,220
Payments to suppliers of goods	44,800
Insurance	360
Rates	450
Advertising	1,240
Light and heat	480
Drawings	3,800

The following is a summary of his *cash* account for the year ended 31 March 2009:

	£
Receipts from goods sold	57,150
Cash paid into bank	41,200
Drawings	7,000
Wage payments	8,100
Repairs and decorations	100
Carriage outwards	250

Further information was provided on transactions during the year ended 31 March 2009:

a Fixtures and fittings were to be depreciated by 10% per annum at the beginning of the year.

b Insurance had been paid for the period from 1 April 2008 till 30 September 2009.

c A further amount of £350 was still owed for wages.

d Discounts allowed for the year were £450.

e At 31 March 2009 the following balances were provided:

	£
Stock	21,200
Trade debtors	6,100
Trade creditors	6,500

Required

1 Prepare Bodystore's profit and loss account for the year ended 31 March 2009.

2 Prepare Bodystore's balance sheet as at 31 March 2009.

Question 3

The Fotiades brothers own the SouvlakiHat, a casual Greek restaurant, but they do not keep a full set of accounting records. However, the following information has been produced from the restaurant's records:

a Summary of the bank account for the year ended 31 August 2009:

	£		£
1 Sept. 2008 balance b/d	15,820	Purchase of delivery van B	16,000
Sale of private holiday house	40,000	Motor vehicle expenses	1,350
Sale of delivery van A	10,000	Advertising	2,560
Receipts from trade debtors	121,000	Rent and rates	10,200
		Wages	25,000
		Electricity	390
		Payments to suppliers	105,000
		Insurances	550
		Drawings	22,000
		31 Aug. 2009 balance c/d	3,770
	£186,820		£186,820

b Assets and liabilities, other than balance at bank:

As at:	1 Sept. 2008	31 Aug. 2009
	£	£
Trade debtors	12,540	9,500
Trade creditors	10,400	9,880
Delivery vans:		
A – at cost	22,500	–
Provision for dep'n	13,500	–
B – at cost	–	16,000
Provision for dep'n	–	To be determined
Stock in trade	2,700	2,900
Insurances prepaid	1,550	1,300
Rent and rates accruals	500	450

c All receipts are banked and all payments are made from the business bank account.

d Discounts received during the year ended 31 August 2009 from trade creditors amounted to £3,100.

e A trade debt of £540 owing by Meat Suppliers Ltd and included in the trade debtors at 31 August 2009 is to be written off as irrecoverable.

f It is SouvlakiHat's policy to provide depreciation at the rate of 20 percent per annum on the cost of delivery vans held at the end of each accounting year; no depreciation is provided in the year of sale of a delivery van.

Required

1 Prepare SouvlakiHat's profit and loss account for the year ended 31 August 2009.

2 Prepare SouvlakiHat's balance sheet as at 31 August 2009.

Question 4

Mr Xo owns a retail shop. You prepare annually the profit and loss account and balance sheet from records consisting of a bank statement and a file of unpaid suppliers and outstanding debtors.

The following balances were shown on his balance sheet at 1 August 2008:

	£
Shop fittings (cost £1,250) at net book value	1,000
Stock in hand	150
Trade debtors	350
Cash at bank	500
Cash float in till	50
Shop trade creditors	1,250

The following is a summary of his bank statement for the year ended 31 July 2009:

	£
Takings banked	9,850
Mr Yhow – shopfitter	310
Payments to suppliers	5,440
Postage and stationery	150
Rent of shop to 31 October 2009	1,800
Sundry expenses	80

You obtain the following additional information:

a Takings are banked daily and all suppliers are paid by cheque, but Mr Xo keeps £200 per week for himself, and pays his assistant £250 per week out of the cash takings.

b The work done by Mr Yhow was for new shelving and repairs to existing fittings in the shop. The cost of the new shelves was £250.

c The cash float in the till was considered insufficient and raised to £75.

d Mr Xo took goods for his own use without payment. The selling price of those goods are £255.

e Your charges as the shop's accountant will be £100 for preparing the accounts.

f The outstanding accounts file shows £1,300 due to suppliers, £20 due in respect of sundry expenses, and £120 outstanding debtors.

g Depreciation on shop fittings is provided at 10 percent on cost, a full year's charge being made in year of purchase.

h Stock in hand at 31 July 2009 was £550.

Required

1 Prepare Mr Xo's profit and loss account for the year ended 31 July 2009.

2 Prepare Mr Xo's balance sheet as at 31 July 2009.

Answers

Question 1

Requirement 1

Bank

	£000		£000
Trade debtors	1,200	Balance b/d	15
		Trade creditors	900
		Telephone and internet	90
		Advertising	30
		Accountant's fee	25
		Rent and rates	13
		Public relations service fee	250
Balance c/d	203	Drawings	80
	1,403		1,403

Trade creditors

Bank	900	Balance b/d	150
Balance c/d	190	Purchases	940
	1,090		1,090

Trade debtors

Balance b/d	480	Bank	1,200
Sales	986	Discount allowed	10
		Bad debts	6
		Balance c/d	250
	1,466		1,466

Telephone and internet

Prepayment b/d	34	Profit and loss a/c	84
Bank	90	Prepayment c/d	40
	124		124

Advertising

Prepayment b/d	16	Profit and loss a/c	56
Bank	30		
Accrual c/d	10		
	56		56

Accountant's fee

Bank	25	Accrual b/d	12
Accrual c/d	20	Profit and loss a/c	33
	45		45

Rent and rates

	£000		£000
Bank	13	Accrual b/d	3
		Profit and loss a/c	5
		Prepayment c/d	5
	13		13

Requirement 2

Saturdays
Profit and loss account for the year ended 31 December 2007

	£000	£000
Sales		986
Less Cost of sales		
Stock at 1 Jan. 2007	300	
Add Purchases	940	
	1,240	
Less Stock at 31 Dec. 2007	350	890
Gross profit		96
Less Expenditure		
Telephone and internet	84	
Advertising	56	
Accountant's fee	33	
Rent and rates	5	
Public relations service fee	250	
Discount allowed	10	
Bad debts	6	
Depreciation	50	494
Net loss		398

Requirement 3

Saturdays
Balance sheet as at 31 December 2007

	£000	£000
Fixed assets	500	
Less Accumulated depreciation (150 + 50)	200	300
Current assets		
Stock	350	
Prepayments (40 + 5)	45	
Trade debtors	250	645
Less Current liabilities		
Bank	203	
Trade creditors	190	
Accrued expenses (20 + 10)	30	423
Net assets		522
Owner's equity		
Capital balance at 1 Jan. 2007		1,000
Less Net loss		398
		602
Less Drawings		80
Balance at 31 Dec. 2007		522

Question 2

Workings

(i)

Bodystore
Balance sheet as at 1 April 2008

	£
Fixtures	5,500
Premises	85,000
Trade debtors	5,700
Bank	19,854
Cash	100
Stock	25,000
	141,154
Less Shop creditors	7,440
Capital at 1 April 2008	133,714

(ii)

Bank

	£		£
Balance b/d	19,854	Suppliers	44,800
Takings banked	41,200	Insurance	360
Interest from private		Rates	450
investment	1,220	Advertising	1,240
		Light and heat	480
		Drawings	3,800
		Balance c/d	11,144
	62,274		62,274

Cash

Balance b/d	100	Bank	41,200
Takings	57,150	Drawings	7,000
		Wages	8,100
		Repairs and decorations	100
		Carriage outwards	250
		Balance c/d	600
	57,250		57,250

Trade creditors

Bank	44,800	Balance b/d	7,440
Balance c/d	6,500	Purchases	43,860
	51,300		51,300

Trade debtors

Balance b/d	5,700	Bank	57,150
Sales	58,000	Discounts allowed	450
		Balance c/d	6,100
	63,700		63,700

Requirement 1

Bodystore
Profit and loss account for the year ended 31 March 2009

	£	£
Sales		58,000
Less Cost of sales		
Stock at 1 April 2008	25,000	
Add Purchases	43,860	
	75,890	
Less Stock at 31 March 2009	21,200	47,660
Gross profit		10,340
Less Expenditure		
Insurance (360 – 120)	240	
Rates	450	
Advertising	1,240	
Light and heat	480	
Wages (8,100 + 350)	8,450	
Repairs and decorations	100	
Carriage outwards	250	
Discounts allowed	450	
Depreciation of fixtures (5,500 × 10%)	550	12,210
Net loss		(1,870)

Requirement 2

Bodystore
Balance sheet as at 31 March 2009

	£	£
Fixed assets		
Premises		85,000
Fixtures and fittings		5,500
Less Accumulated depreciation		550
		89,950
Current assets		
Stock	21,200	
Debtors	6,100	
Prepaid insurance	120	
Bank	11,144	
Cash	600	39,164
Less Current liabilities		
Creditors	6,500	
Accrued wages	350	6,850
Net assets		122,264

Owner's equity

Capital balance at 1 April 2008	133,714
New capital introduced	1,220
Less Loss for year	1,870
	133,064
Less Drawings (3,800 + 7,000)	10,800
Balance at 31 March 2009	122,264

Question 3

Workings

i.
SouvlakiHat
Balance sheet as at 1 September 2008

Assets

Motor vans (£22,500 − £13,500)		9,000
Stock		2,700
Debtors		12,540
Prepayments		1,550
Bank		15,820
		41,610
Less Liabilities		
Creditors	10,400	
Accrued expenses	500	10,900
Capital at 1 Sept. 2008		30,710

ii.
Trade creditors

	£		£
Bank	105,000	Balance b/d	10,400
Discount received	3,100	Purchases	107,580
Balance c/d	9,880		
	117,980		117,980

Trade debtors

	£		£
Balance b/d	12,540	Bank	121,000
Sales	117,960	Bad debts	540
		Balance c/d	8,960
		(9,500 − 540)	
	130,500		130,500

iii. Rent and rates £10,200 − £500 + £450 = £10,150

iv. Insurances £550 + £1,550 − £1,300 = £800

v. *Delivery vans*:

Depreciation expense of van B: 20% × £16,000 = £3,200

Profit on sale of van A: £10,000 − (£22,500 − £13,500) = £1,000

Requirement 1

SouvlakiHat

Profit and loss account for the year ended 31 August 2009

	£	£
Sales		117,960
Less Cost of sales		
Stock at 1 Sept. 2008	2,700	
Add Purchases	107,580	
	75,890	
Less Stock at 31 Aug. 2009	2,900	107,380
Gross profit		10,580
Add Discount received		3,100
profit on sale of van		1,000
		14,680
Less Expenditure		
Rent and rates	10,150	
Wages	25,000	
Motor vehicle expenses	1,350	
Advertising	2,560	
Electricity	390	
Insurances	800	
Bad debts	540	
Depreciation on vans	3,200	43,990
Net loss		29,310

Requirement 2

SouvlakiHat

Balance sheet as at 31 August 2009

	£	£
Fixed assets		
Delivery van B at cost		16,000
Less Depreciation for year		3,200
Net book value		12,800
Current assets		
Stock	2,900	
Trade debtors (9,500 – 540)	8,960	
Prepayments	1,300	
Bank	3,770	16,930
Less Current liabilities		
Trade creditors	9,880	
Accrued expenses	450	10,330
Net assets		19,400
Owner's equity		
Capital balance at 1 Sept. 2008		30,710
Add Capital introduced		40,000
Less Loss for year		29,310
		41,400
Less Drawings		22,000
Balance at 31 Aug. 2009		19,400

Question 4

Workings

i.

Mr Xo
Balance sheet as at 1 August 2008

	£
Shop fittings	1,000
Stock	150
Trade debtors	350
Bank	500
Cash	50
	2,050
Less Shop creditors	1,250
Capital at 1 August 2008	800

ii.

Bank

	£		£
Balance b/d	500	Shop fittings	310
Takings banked	9,850	Suppliers	5,440
		Postage and stationery	150
		Rent	1,800
		Sundry expenses	80
		Balance c/d	2,570
	10,350		10,350

Cash

	£		£
Balance b/d	50	Bank	9,850
Takings		Drawings (£200 × 52)	10,400
(balancing figure)	33,275	Wages (£250 × 52)	13,000
		Balance c/d	75
	33,325		33,325

Trade creditors

	£		£
Bank	5,440	Balance b/d	1,250
Balance c/d	1,300	Purchases	5,490
	6,740		6,740

Trade debtors

	£		£
Balance b/d	350	Bank	33,275
Sales	33,045	Balance c/d	120
	33,395		33,395

iii. Depreciation = 10% × (£1,250 + £250) = £150
Aggregate depreciation = £1,250 − £1,000 + £150 = £400

Requirement 1

Mr Xo
Profit and loss account for the year ended 31 July 2009

	£	£
Sales (33,045 + 255)		33,300
Less Cost of sales		
Stock at 1 August 2008	150	
Add Purchases	5,490	
	75,890	
Less Stock at 31 July 2009	550	5,090
Gross profit		28,210
Less Expenditure		
Mr Yhow – Repairs to fittings (310 – 250)	60	
Postage and stationery	150	
Rent	1,440	
Sundry expenses (80 + 20)	100	
Wages	13,000	
Depreciation on fittings	150	
Accountancy charges	100	15,000
Net profit		13,210

Requirement 2

Mr Xo
Balance sheet as at 31 July 2009

	£	£
Fixed assets		
Shop fittings at cost (1,250 + 250)		1,500
Less Accumulated depreciation		400
		1,100
Current assets		
Stock	550	
Debtors	120	
Prepaid rent	360	
Bank	2,570	
Cash	75	3,675
Less Current liabilities		
Creditors	1,300	
Accrued sundry expenses	20	
Accrued accountant's charges	100	1,420
Net assets		3,355
Owner's equity		
Capital balance at 1 August 2008		800
Add Profit for year		13,210
		14,010
Less Drawings (10,400 + 255)		10,655
Balance at 31 July 2009		3,355

Chapter 7

Partnerships

This chapter covers briefly the following topics:

- Partnership accounts
- Changes in the structure of a partnership
- Dissolution (liquidation/winding up) of partnerships
- Conversion of a partnership to a limited company

Partnership accounts

The main difference between the accounts of a partnership and those of a sole trader is the need to keep track of the equity stake of each of the partners. In other words, the equity side of a partnership's balance sheet is more complicated and, for this reason, two more accounts are introduced:

- a CURRENT account for EACH partner
- a PROFIT and LOSS APPROPRIATION account

The **capital account** for *each* partner contains *only* the *original capital* put into the business *PLUS* any further capital introduced at a later date *MINUS* any withdrawals of capital made by any of the partners.

Current account for *each* partner

The balance on a partner's current account is likely to fluctuate during the accounting year. The partner will draw money (or goods) regularly from the partnership to pay for his/her living expenses and maybe an interest will be charged on the partner's drawings. The drawings and the interest on drawings will be *debited* to his/her current account.

On the other hand, the partner will be entitled to a share of the partnership's profits and this will be *credited* to his/her current account (*note*: if a loss is made during the year, then the partner's share of the residual loss will be debited). Similarly, any interest given on capital invested, partners' salaries, and an interest charged on a loan made by a partner to the partnership will all be *credited* to partners' current accounts.

It is worth remembering that the double entry for the items in the partners' current accounts is on the opposite side of the profit and loss appropriation account, as we will see below.

The T-account of the *partners' current accounts* is as follows (assuming a partnership of A, B and C):

Partner A, B and C current accounts

	A	B	C		A	B	C
Drawings	...	...	...	Bal b/d	...	...	...
Interest charged				Interest on capital	...	...	...
on drawings	...	...	...	Salaries	...	...	...
Bal c/d	...	...	...	Interest on loan			
				to the partnership	...	...	...
				Share of the profit	...	...	...
				Bal b/d	...	...	...

Profit and loss appropriation account

In preparing the partnership's final accounts, the profit and loss account contains exactly the same entries as that of a sole trader. However, in contrast with the sole trader, whose retained profits earned each year are simply added to the capital balance of the sole trader's business, in a partnership things are not as simple.

In a partnership, after the profit and loss account has been prepared and the net profit (or loss) earned by the partnership has been calculated, a *profit and loss appropriation account* must be prepared to determine the allocation of that profit (or loss) between the partners.

If partners have agreed to charge themselves interest on any drawings made from the partnership, then such interest is debited to the partner's current account and *credited* to the appropriation account, increasing in this way the profit available for sharing between the partners.

If partners are paid a salary, then it is credited to the partner's current account and taken out of the 'pool' available for appropriation (i.e. the appropriation account is *debited*). Similarly, if partners are entitled to interest on their capital account balances and interest to any loans they have made to the partnership, then each partner is credited with the interest (on capital and loan) and again the 'pool' is reduced appropriately (i.e. the appropriation account is *debited*).

Finally, the remaining amount (i.e. the residual 'pool' of profits or losses) is shared among the partners in the agreed profit sharing ratio.

It is worth remembering that the *double entry* for the items in the profit and loss appropriation account is on the opposite side of the partners' current accounts.

The T-account of the profit and loss appropriation account is as follows:

Profit and loss appropriation account

	A	B	C				
Loan interest				Net profit b/d		. . .	
A	. . .			Interest on drawings			
B	. . .			A		. . .	
C	. . .	. . .		B		. . .	
Salaries				C		. . .	. . .
A	. . .						
B	. . .						
C	. . .	. . .					
Interest on capital							
A	. . .						
B	. . .						
C	. . .	. . .					
Share of residual profit							
A	. . .						
B	. . .						
C	. . .	. . .					
		xxx					xxx

Changes in the structure of a partnership

The structure of a partnership may change if new partners are admitted or existing partners retire/leave. This is likely to cause accounting problems if the books of the partnership do not fully reflect the value of the partnership. Such a situation is very common, for example when a retiring partner wants to withdraw his/her share of the partnership assets but the partnership accounts prepared under the *historical cost* convention are not likely to reflect the *current value* of his/her share of the business.

The usual solution is to make adjustments so that partners' capital accounts reflect the current/market value of both the partnership's tangible and intangible assets, such as goodwill. In other words, assets and liabilities must be revalued to their current/market value and, in effect, this means that there will be unrealised holding gains or losses which will need to be recorded in the books.

When a new partner is admitted or an existing partner retires/leaves then, by revaluing the assets to their current value, each partner's capital account is *credited* with their share of the unrealised gains (or *debited* with their share of the unrealised losses).

Finally, a value of goodwill needs to recognised as the partners have created it and therefore it belongs to them. The goodwill is recognised only when all other assets have been revalued in their current values. As such, no goodwill exists in the partnership accounts before, and the creation of goodwill has an effect directly on the partner's capital accounts.

Revaluation of assets

The recognition of unrealised holding gains or losses through the revaluation process of assets (and liabilities) is done by opening a *revaluation account*.

The double entries are as follows:

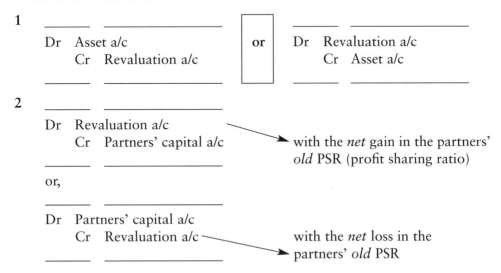

1

Dr   Asset a/c
  Cr   Revaluation a/c

or

Dr   Revaluation a/c
  Cr   Asset a/c

2

Dr   Revaluation a/c
  Cr   Partners' capital a/c   → with the *net* gain in the partners' *old* PSR (profit sharing ratio)

or,

Dr   Partners' capital a/c
  Cr   Revaluation a/c   → with the *net* loss in the partners' *old* PSR

The revaluation account takes the following format (assuming a partnership of A and B):

Revaluation account

Decrease in assets	Increase in assets
and	and
Increase in liabilities	Decrease in liabilities
Gain on revaluation	**Loss on revaluation**
Capital a/c of partner A	Capital a/c of partner A
Capital a/c of partner B	Capital a/c of partner B

Goodwill

The accounting entries on a change in the partnership will depend on whether goodwill is to *remain* in the accounts of the new partnership. There are two methods of treating goodwill on a change in a partnership:

1 *If goodwill is to be* included *in the accounts*
   Open a goodwill account by debiting goodwill and crediting the old partners' capital accounts in their *old* profit-sharing ratio (PSR). Goodwill is then to be recorded as an asset in the balance sheet of the new partnership and

maintained in the business. The goodwill is then also amortised (i.e. depreciated) over its useful economic life.

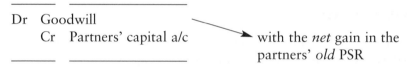

Dr   Goodwill
    Cr   Partners' capital a/c   with the *net* gain in the
                                           partners' *old* PSR

2 *If goodwill is* not *to be included in the accounts*
Open a goodwill account (and immediately close it, i.e. no balance to be carried down). The process is as follows: goodwill is to be recorded first and credited to the old partners' capital accounts in their *old* profit-sharing ratio (as in the above method).

Then, the goodwill account is to be balanced off by crediting the goodwill account and debiting all the partners' capital accounts in their *new* profit-sharing ratio.

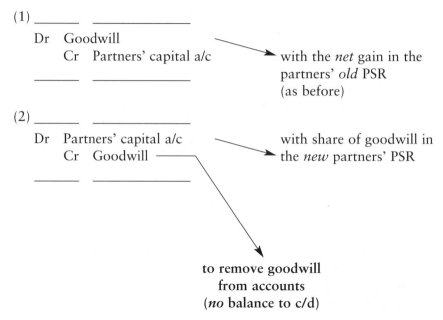

(1)
    Dr   Goodwill
        Cr   Partners' capital a/c   with the *net* gain in the
                                   partners' *old* PSR
                                   (as before)

(2)
    Dr   Partners' capital a/c   with share of goodwill in
        Cr   Goodwill   the *new* partners' PSR

to remove goodwill
from accounts
(*no* balance to c/d)

Note: this method has the effect of charging the new partner with a premium (or a bonus), in that his/her capital introduced has been reduced by his/her share of the goodwill. This premium represents the purchase by the new partner of his/her share of goodwill.

Dissolution (liquidation/winding up) of partnerships

The term dissolution of partnerships refers to a situation where all the partners wish to leave, and thus the activities of the partnership come to an end.

When a partnership comes to an end, the following basic steps need to be considered:

1 Prepare a set of final accounts from the end of the previous accounting year to the date of dissolution.

2 Sell the assets (or allow partners to take over some or all of the assets) and collect money from trade debtors.

3 Pay the partnership's liabilities in the following order: trade creditors, loans and then any partners' loans.

4 Current accounts are closed and transferred to partners' capital accounts.

5 Finally, close the partners' capital accounts and disburse the remaining cash to the partners in their profit-sharing ratio.

The achievement of the above steps requires the preparation of the following three accounts:

- the realisation account;
- the partners' capital accounts;
- the cash/bank account.

The *realisation account* is similar to the revaluation account as it includes any profit or loss that arises from the dissolution of a partnership. This account takes the following form:

Realisation account

Transfer of *all* assets (except cash or bank) at book values	Provisions for depreciation of plant assets
Payment of expenses for dissolution	Provision for bad debts
Any interest paid for early settlement of loans	Cash receipts upon dissolution (e.g. from sale of assets and/or collection of trade debtors)
Any loss on settlement of liabilities	Any gain on settlement of liabilities (e.g. discount received by trade creditor)
	Any assets taken over by partners at the agreed value (debit partner's capital account)
Gain on realisation (balancing figure)	Loss on realisation (balancing figure)

The journal entries to record the realisation process are as follows:

Dr   Realisation a/c   Transfer of assets'
    Cr   Sundry assets a/c (except cash and bank)   book values

Dr   Bank a/c   Receipts from sale
    Cr   Realisation a/c   of assets

Dr   Capital a/c   Assets taken over
    Cr   Realisation a/c   by partners

Dr   Realisation a/c   Expenses
    Cr   Bank a/c

Dr   Creditor a/c   Any gains
    Cr   Realisation a/c   (e.g. discount)
                                                            on settlement

Dr   Realisation a/c   Share of profit on
    Cr   Capital a/c   realisation

Dr   Capital a/c   Share of loss on
    Cr   Realisation a/c   realisation

Conversion of a partnership to a limited company

There are two possibilities of converting a partnership into a limited company:
(a) when a partnership is transferred to a company, and (b) when a partnership
is sold to an existing company.

Transfer to a company

A partnership could be taken over by another business and converted to a limited company. Upon conversion, the partnership's assets and liabilities are revalued, goodwill is created and capital is paid off by an issue of shares. The partnership is converted to a company as a going-concern.

The accounting entries for the new company are as follows:

> Dr The individual assets acquired from the partnership
> > Cr The individual liabilities, at the agreed valuations
> > Cr Share capital and share premium account

Sale of partnership to an existing company

When a partnership is to be sold to an existing company, we may face one of two cases:

> Case 1: Fair values are given for the assets acquired and any liabilities taken over but the *market value* of shares issued in consideration is unknown.

In this case, the total fair value of net assets determines the fair value of any shares issued as consideration. Any difference between the nominal value of shares issued and the fair value of net assets is credited to a share premium account.

> Case 2: Fair value of shares in consideration and the fair value of net assets acquired are given.

In this case, goodwill is the difference between the fair value of consideration given and the total fair value of the separable net assets acquired.

Short questions

Question

Dang, Ding and Dong are partners sharing residual profits in the ratio 3:2:1. The partnership agreement provides for a salary for Ding of £35,000 per annum and for interest on capital at the rate of 10 percent per annum. The balances on partners' capital accounts during the year were as follows: Dang £50,000, Ding £45,000 and Dong £40,000, and the partnership's net profit for 2008 was £128,000.

1 Calculate Dong's share of residual profits for 2008.

2 Calculate the total of the appropriations credited to Ding's current account in 2008.

Answer

	Dang £	Ding £	Dong £	Total £
Profit for 2008				128,000
Partner's salary		(35,000)		(35,000)
Interest on capital	(5,000)	(4,500)	(4,000)	(13,500)
	(5,000)	(39,500)	(4,000)	79,500
Residual profits				
shared 3:2:1	(39,750)	(26,500)	(13,250)	(79,500)
	44,750	66,000	17,250	0

1 Dong's share of residual profits for 2008 is £13,250.

2 The total of the appropriations credited to Ding's current account in 2008 is £66,000.

Question

Alf and Bert are partners in a newsagent business. They share residual profits in the ratio 3:2 after interest on partners' capital of 8 percent per annum and interest on partners' drawings of 11 percent per annum. Their capital balances in 2008 were £30,000 and £25,000 respectively, and the current account balances were £4,000 and £1,500 respectively. The average balances on their drawings accounts were £40,000 and £45,000. The partnership's net profit for 2008 was £94,000.

1 Calculate the balance of residual profits available for appropriation in sharing ratio.

2 Calculate the net amount of all the sums transferred from the appropriation account to the current account of Alf.

3 Show the capital structure of the partnership.

Answer

	Alf £	Bert £	Total £
Profit for 2008			94,000
Interest on capital	(2,400)	(2,000)	(4,400)
Interest on drawings	4,400	4,950	9,350
	2,000	2,950	98,950
Residual profits shared 3:2	(59,370)	(39,580)	(98,950)
	57,370	36,630	0

1 The balance of residual profits available for appropriation in sharing ratio is £98,950.

2 The net amount of all the sums transferred from the appropriation account to the current account of Alf is £57,370.

Partners' current accounts

	Alf £	Bert £	Alf £	Bert £	
Drawings	40,000	45,000	4,000	1,500	Bal b/d
Interest on					Interest on
Drawings	4,400	4,950	2,400	2,000	Capital
			59,370	39,580	Share on profit
Bal c/d	21,370	–	–	6,870	Bal c/d
	65,770	49,950	65,770	49,950	
Bal b/d	–	6,870	21,370	–	Bal b/d

3 Therefore, the capital structure of the partnership would be as follows:

	Alf £	Bert £	Total £
Capital accounts	30,000	25,000	55,000
Current accounts	21,370	(6,870)	14,500
	51,370	31,870	69,500

Question

Iliana and Ilias commenced a partnership on 1 January 2009, each contributing capital of €25,000, and agreed to share profits equally. The partnership's net profit is €9,000 for the period to 30 June 2009 and on that date they are joined in partnership by Iliadae who contributes capital of €30,000. At that time goodwill was valued at €15,000, and the three partners agree to share profits equally. They do not wish to retain goodwill in the partnership's accounts.

What is the balance on Iliadae's capital account at 1 July 2009?

Answer

Partners' capital accounts

	Ilias €	Iliana €	Iliadae €	Ilias €	Iliana €	Iliadae €	
Goodwill	5,000	5,000	5,000	25,000	25,000	–	Bank
				4,500	4,500		Profit
Bal c/d	32,000	32,000	25,000	–	–	30,000	Bank
				7,500	7,500	–	Goodwill
	37,000	37,000	30,000	37,000	37,000	30,000	
				32,000	32,000	25,000	Bal b/d

Therefore, the balance on Iliadae's capital account at 1 July 2009 is €25,000.

Questions

Question 1

Stan and Stuart, partners in a manufacturing business, share profits and losses equally. They have the following partnership agreement:

	Stan	Stuart
	£	£
Salaries per annum:	70,000	60,000
Interest on fixed capitals (per annum)	10%	10%

Their capital and current balances as at 1 June 2008 and their drawings by 31 May 2009 were respectively:

Capital account on	30,000	17,000
Current account (both on credit)	8,500	5,550
Drawings per month	600	500

The following financial information is available for the year ended 31 May 2009, after the preparation of the profit and loss account:

	£
Net profit for year (before appropriation)	150,000
Motor vehicles at cost	25,000
Provision for depreciation of motor vehicles	4,800
Bank	45,000
Cash	5,000
Trade debtors	15,800
Trade creditors	3,200
Shop premises at cost	90,000
Stock	25,000

Required
1 Prepare a profit and loss appropriation account for the ear ended 31 May 2009.
2 Prepare the current account for *each* partner as at 31 May 2009.
3 Prepare a balance sheet as at 31 May 2009.

Question 2

Dixon, Cowell and Cooper are in partnership sharing profits and losses in the ratio 2:2:1 respectively.

During the year ended 31 December 2007 the net profit of the firm was €30,538. You are also given the following information:

	Dixon	Cowell	Cooper
	€	€	€
Partners' drawings	6,000	5,500	3,900
Interest on partners' drawings	180	165	117

Interest is allowed on partners' capitals at the rate of 6 percent per annum. Cowell is entitled to a salary of €9,000 per annum. The partners agreed that Dixon should

150

withdraw €10,000 from her capital at 1 July 2007 and that Cooper should contribute a similar amount as at that date.

The balances on the partners' accounts at 1 January 2007 were:

	Capital accounts (all credit balances)	Current accounts
	€	€
Dixon	45,000	1,000 credit balance
Cowell	49,000	900 debit balance
Cooper	40,000	500 debit balance

Required

1 Prepare the partnership profit and loss appropriation account.
2 Show the partners' capital for the year ended 31 December 2007.
3 Prepare the partners' current accounts for the year ended 31 December 2007.

Question 3

Harisson Ford and Al Pacino, two actors, decided to form a partnership. They agreed that they would have their own regional selling areas and be responsible for their own sales. The partnership agreement provided that:

a Each partner is to be credited with a commission of 10 percent on his own annual sales. The commission is to be treated as an appropriation of profits.
b All other expenses would be treated as expenses of the whole business.
c Profits and losses are to be shared equally.

Harisson (H) and Al (A) commenced joint operations on 1 January 2008 by providing the following capital:

H	Cash £10,000	A	Cash £10,000
	Stock of goods for sale £4,000		Stock of goods for sale £5,000
	Office £11,000		Office equipment £5,000
	Motor vehicle £9,000		Motor vehicle £9,000

For the year ended 31 December 2008, the following financial information is available:

		£
i.	Advertising	2,600
	Telephone and internet	1,000
	Purchases	91,800
	Wages	14,500
	Sales by H	74,300
	Sales by A	56,100
	Rent and rates	10,600
	Carriage inwards	2,100
	Heating and lighting	800
	Accountant's fee	500
	Drawings H	8,050
	Drawings A	5,750
	Sales returns to H	1,300
	Sales returns to A	1,100

		£
ii.	Telephone and internet owing at 31 December 2008	100
	Advertising paid in advance at 31 December 2008	400

iii. Motor vehicles are to be depreciated by 20 percent per annum
Office equipment is to be similarly depreciated by 10 percent per annum

iv. Closing balances at 31 December 2008:

	£
Cash	300
Bank	7,800
Trade debtors	17,900
Trade creditors	14,700
Stock	25,000

Required

1 Prepare a profit and loss and appropriation account for the year ended 31 December 2008,

2 Show the current account for *each* partner as at 31 December 2008,

3 Prepare a balance sheet as at 31 December 2008.

Question 4

Elisabeth and Philip are in partnership, sharing profits and losses in the ratio 2:1. The following trial balance was prepared as at 29 February 2008:

	Dr	Cr
	$	$
Stock 1 March 2007	5,340	
Purchases and sales	11,250	28,010
Trade debtors and trade creditors	5,000	2,500
Rent, rates and insurance	650	
Fixture and fittings	990	
Bad debts	400	
Partners' capital accounts as at 1 March 2007		
– Elisabeth		5,000
– Philip		3,000
Partners' current accounts, 1 March 2007		
– Elisabeth		520
– Philip		410
Drawings – Elisabeth	3,100	
– Philip	3,900	
Bank	2,950	
Cash	190	
Wages and salaries	4,400	
Discounts	750	400
General office expenses	920	
	39,840	39,840

The following matters relate to the partnership accounts:

a No interest is to be allowed on capital accounts.

b Philip is entitled to a partnership salary of $5,290 but no entries have been made regarding this.

c The partners' capital accounts are to remain fixed at the figures shown in the trial balance. All other transactions concerning partners are to be made in the partners' current accounts.

d Stock at 29 February 2008 is $4,340.

e Amount of $200 for wages and salaries accrued at 29 February 2008.

f No provision is to be made for depreciation.

g Amount of $50 for rates prepaid at 29 February 2008.

Required

1 Prepare a profit and loss and appropriation account for the year ended 29 February 2008.

2 Prepare a balance sheet as at 29 February 2008.

Question 5

Chip, Dale and Duck are partners of a trading firm and share profits and losses in the ratio 3:2:1. The firm's balance sheet on 31 December 2006 was:

	£	£
Fixed assets		
Freehold premises		25,000
Motor vehicles at cost less depreciation		19,000
		44,000
Current assets		
Stock	12,000	
Debtors	15,000	
Balance at bank	11,000	38,000
Current liabilities		
Creditors	8,000	8,000
Net assets		74,000
Partners' capital accounts	£	
Chip	36,000	
Dale	24,000	
Duck	12,000	72,000
Partners' current accounts		
Chip	2,400	
Dale	Dr (1,600)	
Duck	1,200	2,000	74,000

Dale retired from the Partnership on 1 January 2007 and agreed to leave half the final balance on his capital account as a short-term loan to the firm. The remainder was paid to him in cash immediately.

Chip and Duck had agreed to continue in partnership sharing profits and losses in the same proportions as before. Unrecorded goodwill on 1 January was valued at £18,000.

Required

1 Prepare the capital Accounts of Chip, Dale and Duck as at 1 January 2007.

2 Show Dale's loan account as at 1 January 2007.

Question 6

Bill, George and Obama were partners with capitals of £80,000, £100,000 and £20,000 respectively. They shared profits and losses in proportion to their capitals. George retired from the partnership on 31 December 2007. The partnership deed provided that, in the event of dissolution, goodwill would be valued at three years' purchase of the average partnership profits of the last four years. These profits were £22,900, £34,100, £19,600 and £23,400. The balance sheet of the partnership on 31 December 2008, prior to dissolution, was:

	£	£
Assets		
Sundry assets	90,000	
Cash	150,000	240,000
Liabilities		
Sundry creditors	40,000	40,000
Net assets		200,000
Capital – Bill	80,000	
Capital – George	100,000	
Capital – Obama	20,000	200,000

By agreement, George immediately took out of the business the car he had been using (book value £10,000) and, on 17 February 2008, he was paid to clear his capital account including his share of goodwill.

Required

1 Prepare a statement showing the calculations for the value of goodwill.

2 Prepare a goodwill account for the old partnership.

3 Prepare the balance sheet for the new partnership of Bill and Obama as at 1 January 2008.

Question 7

Farkha, Sakhira and Sab are in partnership sharing profits and losses, Farkha 5/12, Sakhira 1/3 and Sab 1/4. On 1 September 2009 Sakhira retired from the partnership and at the same date Nazick was admitted to the partnership, introducing cash of €50,000. From this date, profits are to be shared equally between the three new partners and, in view of this, Sab agreed to pay a further €12,000 into the partnership as capital.

The balance sheet at 31 August 2009 is as follows:

	€	€
Fixed assets		
Buildings		100,000
Furniture and fixtures		45,000
		145,000
Current assets		
Stock	120,000	
Trade debtors	75,000	
Bank	95,000	290,000
Liabilities: Trade creditors	60,000	60,000
Net assets		375,000
Capital accounts		
Farkha	150,000	
Sakhira	120,000	
Sab	70,000	340,000
Current accounts		
Farkha	9,000	
Sakhira	15,000	
Sab	11,000	35,000
		375,000

The following adjustments should be made before preparing a revised opening balance sheet of the partnership on 1 September 2009:

a Goodwill of the partnership as at 31 August 2009 is agreed at €39,960. Goodwill is not to be included in the accounts.

b Property is to be revalued at €120,000 and fixtures are to be revalued at €49,000.

c Stock is considered to be shown at a fair market value in the accounts. A provision for doubtful debts of €1,708 is to be created.

d Professional fees of €500 relating to the change in partnership structure are to be regarded as an expense of the year to 31st August 2009, but were not included in the profit and loss account of that year. They are expected to be paid in October 2009.

e On retirement, Sakhira is to be paid a sum of €55,000. Sakhira has agreed to leave any remaining amount owing to her in the partnership as a loan. Sakhira's loan carries interest of 12 percent per annum, and is to be repaid in full after two years.

f All balances on current accounts are to be transferred to capital accounts. All balances on capital accounts in excess of €20,000 after this transfer are to be recorded in loan accounts carrying interest of 12 percent per annum.

Required

1 Prepare the partnership's revaluation account.

2 Prepare the partnership's bank account.

3 Prepare the partners' capital accounts.

4 Prepare an opening balance sheet for the partnership on 1 September 2009, following completion of the above arrangements.

Question 8

Marshall, Brendan and Nick are partners and sharing profits or losses in the ratio of 2:1:1 respectively. On 31 July 2009, they agree to dissolve the partnership. Their balance sheet as at 31 July 2009 (i.e. the date of dissolution) was as listed below:

Balance sheet as at 31 July 2009

		£		£
Capital:	Marshall	20,000	Premises	28,500
	Brendan	14,000	Machinery	16,700
	Nick	11,500	Vehicles	3,640
Loan		3,100	Trade debtors	11,950
Trade creditors		4,500	Stock	11,000
Mortgage		18,500		
Bank overdraft		190		

The terms of the dissolution agreement are as follows:

a) Stock was taken over by Nick at its market price of £12,900 less 10 percent.

b) Marshall is to assume responsibility for the trade creditors.

c) Marshall is to take over the premises at a revalued figure of £38,000 and to pay off the mortgage.

d) Marshall also takes one half of the machinery for £9,500 and the trade debtors to the extent of £8,550 for £7,500.

e) Brendan is to take over the vehicles at book value less 20 percent and the remaining machinery at book value less 10 percent.

f) The remaining trade debtors were sold to a debt collection agency for £2,300.

g) The loan was fully repaid.

h) Expenses amounting to £679 were paid.

i) Final balances of the partners' capital accounts are settled by payments of cash.

Required

1 Prepare the partnership's realisation account.

2 Prepare the partnership's bank account.

3 Prepare the partners' capital accounts.

Question 9

Bonnie and Clyde have been in partnership for several years sharing profits equally. The partnership accounting year-end is 31 December. On 20 February 2009, they have decided to dissolve the partnership. After preparing the profit and loss account for the period 1 January 2009 to 20 February 2009, the balance sheet as at the latter date is as follows:

	$	$	$
Motor vehicles		45,000	
Less Provision for depreciation		12,200	32,800
Stock		5,700	
Trade debtors	21,800		
Less Provision for doubtful debts	1,100	20,700	
Prepaid expenses		290	26,690
Less Liabilities			
Trade creditors		25,490	
Bank overdraft		5,000	
Bank loan		9,000	
Accrued expenses		3,000	42,490
			17,000
Capital – Bonnie		9,000	
– Clyde		5,000	14,000
Current account – Bonnie		5,000	
– Clyde (on debit)		(2,000)	3,000
			17,000

One of the motor vehicles was taken over by Clyde at an agreed valuation of $10,000. The remainder of the vehicles were sold for $15,500. The stock realised $6,500 and $17,800 was received from trade debtors. A refund of the full amount of prepaid expenses was also received. Trade creditors were paid $20,900 in full settlement. The bank loan was fully repaid, including an interest penalty for early settlement of $250. Accrued expenses were also fully paid off. Expenses for dissolving the partnership amounted to $1,500. The partnership also sold its business name and a list of its customers to a competitor for $3,000.

Required

1 Prepare the partnership's realisation account.

2 Prepare the partnership's bank account.

3 Prepare the partners' capital accounts.

Question 10

Obama and Hilary are in partnership, sharing profits and losses in the ratio 3:2. At 1 May 2008 they agree to sell their business to Save the Planet Ltd. The partnership balance sheet was as follows:

Balance sheet as at 30 April 2008

	£	£
Fixed assets		
Freehold premises	65,000	
Plant and machinery	49,000	
Fixtures and fittings	9,200	
		123,200
Current assets		
Stock	17,000	
Sundry debtors	21,700	
Balance at bank	12,300	
		51,000
Current liabilities		
Sundry creditors	13,200	
		13,200
Net assets		161,000
Capital accounts		
Obama	96,390	
Hilary	56,610	
		153,000
Current accounts		
Obama	3,400	
Hilary	4,600	
		8,000
		161,000

Save the Planet Ltd was a new company formed to purchase the above partnership business. Its authorised share capital is £1,000,000, made up of 300,000 7 percent preference shares of £1 each, and 700,000 ordinary shares of £1 each.

The purchase price was to be £190,000, and the company proposed to settle this amount by the issue at par of 160,000 £1 Ordinary Shares, issued as fully paid, to the partners, the balance of the purchase price to be settled in cash on 20 May 2008. The ordinary share distribution was made in the capital ratio of the partners at 30 April 2008.

The company agreed to take over *all* the assets except the bank account, and also agreed to take over the responsibility for payment of the creditors. The company valued the acquired assets as follows:

	£
Freehold premises	90,000
Plant and machinery	42,000
Fixtures and fittings	5,500
Stock	14,500

The company also agreed to pay £18,000, included in the purchase price, for the total trade debtors taken over.

Required

In the books of the partnership, show the entries necessary, in the following accounts, to close the business:

1 realisation account;

2 bank account;

3 partners' capital accounts;

4 the opening balance sheet of the new company as at 1 May 2008.

Answers

Question 1

Requirement 1

Profit and loss appropriation account for year ended 31 May 2009

	£		£
Salaries		Net profit b/d	150,000
– Stan	70,000		
– Stuart	60,000		
Interest on capital			
– Stan	3,000		
– Stuart	1,700		
Share of residual profits			
– Stan	7,650		
– Stuart	7,650		
	150,000		150,000

Requirement 2

Partners' current accounts

	Stan £	Stuart £		Stan £	Stuart £
Drawings	7,200	6,000	Bal b/d	8,500	5,500
			Salaries	70,000	60,000
			Interest on capital	3,000	1,700
Bal c/d	81,950	68,850	Share of profits	7,650	7,650
	89,150	74,850		89,150	74,850
			Bal b/d	81,950	68,850

159

Requirement 3

<h3 style="text-align:center">Balance sheet as at 31 May 2009</h3>

	£	£	£
Fixed assets			
Shop premises		90,000	
Motor Vehicles	25,000		
Less Provision for depreciation	4,800		
		20,200	
			110,200
Current assets			
Stock		25,000	
Debtors		15,800	
Bank		45,000	
Cash		5,000	
			90,800
Current liabilities			
Trade Creditors			3,200
Net assets			197,800

	£	£	£
Capital accounts			
Stan	30,000		
Stuart	17,000	47,000	
Current accounts			
Stan	81,950		
Stuart	68,850	150,800	
			197,800

Question 2

Requirement 1

Workings:
Interest on capital

Dixon:	(€35,000 × 6%) + (€10,000 × 6% × 6/12)	= €2,400
Cowell:	€49,000 × 6%	= €2,940
Cooper:	(€50,000 × 6%) − (€10,000 × 6% × 6/12)	= €2,700

Profit and loss appropriation account for year 2007

Interest on capital	€		€
Dixon	2,400	Net profit b/d	30,538
Cowell	2,940	*Interest on drawings*	
Cooper	2,700	Dixon	180
Salary – Cowell	9,000	Cowell	165
		Cooper	117
Share of residual profits			
Dixon	5,584		
Cowell	5,584		
Cooper	2,792		
	31,000		31,000

Requirement 2

Partners' capital accounts

	Dixon	Cowell	Cooper		Dixon	Cowell	Cooper
	€	€	€		€	€	€
1 Jul. Bank	10,000			1 Jan. Bal b/d	45,000	49,000	40,000
				1 Jul. Bank			10,000
31 Dec. Bal. c/d	35,000	49,000	50,000		45,000	49,000	50,000
	45,000	49,000	50,000				
				31 Dec. Bal b/d	35,000	49,000	50,000

Requirement 3

Partners' current accounts

	Dixon	Cowell	Cooper		Dixon	Cowell	Cooper
	€	€	€		€	€	€
1 Jan. Bal b/d		900	500	1 Jan. Bal b/d	1,000		
31 Dec. Interest on Drawings	180	165	117	31 Dec. Interest on capital	2,400	2,940	2,700
31 Dec. Drawings	6,000	5,500	3,900	31 Dec. Salary		9,000	
31 Dec. Balance c/d	2,804	10,959	975	31 Dec. Share of Profits	5,584	5,584	2,792
	8,984	17,524	11,792		8,984	17,524	5,492
				31 Dec. Bal b/d	2,804	10,959	975

Question 3

Requirement 1

Profit and loss account for year ended 31 December 2008

		£	
Sales	(£74,300 + 56,100)	130,400	
Less returns	(£1,300 + 1,100)	2,400	
			128,000
COGS:			
Opening stock	(£4,000 + 5,000)	9,000	
Purchases		91,800	
Carriage in		2,100	
		102,900	
Less Closing stock		25,000	
			77,900
Gross profit			50,100
Expenses:			
Advertising		2,200	
Telephone and internet		1,100	
Wages		14,500	
Rent and rates		10,600	
Heating and lighting		800	
Accountant's fee		500	
Depreciation – vehicles [(£9,000 + 9,000) × 20%]		3,600	
Depreciation – office equipment (£5,000 × 10%)		500	
			33,800
Net profit c/d			16,300

Profit and loss appropriation account for year ended 31 December 2008

	£		£
Commission – H	7,300	Net profit b/d	16,300
– A	5,500		
Share of residual profits – H	1,750		
– A	1,750		
	16,300		16,300

Requirement 2

Partners' current accounts

	H £	A £		H £	A £
Drawings	8,050	5,750	Balance b/d	0	0
			Commission on sales	7,300	5,500
Balance c/d	1,000	1,500	Share of profits	1,750	1,750
	9,050	7,250		9,050	7,250
			Balance b/d	1,000	1,500

Requirement 3

Balance sheet as at 31 December 2008

Fixed assets	£	£	£
Office		11,000	
Office equipment	5,000		
Less Provision for depreciation	500	4,500	
Motor vehicles	18,000		
Less Provision for depreciation	3,600		
		14,400	
			29,900
Current assets			
Stock		25,000	
Trade debtors		17,900	
Bank		7,800	
Cash		300	
Advertising prepaid		400	51,400
Current liabilities			
Trade creditors		14,700	
Telephone and internet accrued		100	14,800
Net assets			66,500
Capital accounts			
H		34,000	
A		29,000	63,000
Current accounts			
H		1,000	
A		1,500	2,500
			65,500

Question 4

Requirement 1

Profit and loss account for the year ended 29 February 2008

	$	$	$
Sales		28,010	
COGS			
Opening stock	5,340		
Purchases	11,250		
Closing stock	4,340		
		12,250	
Gross profit			15,760
Discount received			400
Expenses			
Rent, rates, insurance		600	
Discounts allowed		750	
Bad debts		400	
Wages and salaries		4,600	
General expenses		920	
			7,270
Net profit c/d			8,890

Profit and loss appropriation account for year ended 29 February 2008

	$		$
Salaries – Philip	5,290	Net profit b/d	8,890
Share of profits			
– Elisabeth	2,400		
– Philip	1,200		
	8,890		8,890

Requirement 2

Balance sheet as at 29 February 2008

	$	$	$
Fixed assets			
Fixture and fittings			990
Current assets			
Stock		4,340	
Trade debtors		5,000	
Bank		2,950	
Cash		190	
Rates prepaid		50	12,530
Current liabilities			
Trade creditors		2,500	
Wages and salaries accrued		200	2,700
Net assets			10,820

Capital accounts		
– Elisabeth	5,000	
– Philip	3,000	8,000
Current accounts		
– Elisabeth (3,100 – 520 – 2,400)	(180)	
– Philip (3,900 – 410 – 5,290 – 1,200)	3,000	2,820
		10,820

Question 5

Requirement 1

Capital accounts

	Chip £	Dale £	Duck £		Chip £	Dale £	Duck £
Goodwill (out)	10,800	–	7,200	Bal. b/d	36,000	24,000	12,000
Current a/c	–	1,600	–	Goodwill (in)	9,000	6,000	3,000
Loan a/c	–	14,200	–		–	–	–
Cash	–	14,200	–		–	–	–
Bal. c/d	34,200	–	7,800		–	–	–
	45,000	30,000	15,000		45,000	30,000	15,000
				Balances b/d	34,200	–	7,800

Requirement 2

Loan account – Dale

		Capital a/c – Dale	14,200

Question 6

Requirement 1

Goodwill: three years' purchase of the average of the last four year's profits = (£22,900 + 34,100 + 19,600 + 23,400)/4 = £25,000 × 3 = £75,000.

Requirement 2

Goodwill

	£		£
Capital a/c – Bill	30,000	Balance c/d	75,000
Capital a/c – George	37,500		
Capital a/c – Obama	7,500		
	75,000		75,000

Requirement 3

Balance sheet as at 1 January 2008

	£	£
Assets		
Goodwill	75,000	
Sundry assets	80,000	
Cash	160,000	315,000
Liabilities		
Sundry creditors	40,000	
Loan – George	137,500	177,500
Net assets		137,500
Capital – Bill	110,000	
Capital – Obama	27,500	137,500

Question 7

Requirement 1

Revaluation account

	€		€
Provision for doubtful debts	1,708	Buildings	20,000
Professional fees	500	Furniture and fixtures	4,000
Capital – Farkha	9,080		
– Salhira	7,264		
– Sab	5,448		
	24,000		24,000

Requirement 2

Bank account

	€		€
Balance b/d	95,000	Capital – Sakhira	55,000
Capital – Nazick	50,000	Balance c/d	102,000
Capital – Sab	12,000		
	157,000		157,000

Requirement 3

Capital accounts

	Farkha	Sakhira	Sab	Nazick		Farkha	Sakhira	Sab	Nazick
	€	€	€	€		€	€	€	€
Goodwill	13,320	–	13,320	13,320	Bal. b/d	150,000	120,000	70,000	–
Bank	–	55,000	–	–	Current a/c	9,000	15,000	11,000	–
Loan a/c's	151,410	100,584	75,118	16,680	Bank	–	–	12,000	50,000
Balance c/d	20,000	–	20,000	20,000	Share profit	9,080	7,264	5,448	–
					Goodwill	16,650	13,320	9,990	–
	184,730	155,584	108,438	50,000		184,730	155,584	108,438	50,000
					Balance b/d	20,000	–	20,000	20,000

Requirement 4

Farkha, Sab and Nazick
Balance sheet as at 1 September 2009

	€	€	€
Fixed assets			
Buildings		120,000	
Furniture and fixtures		49,000	169,000
Current assets			
Stock		120,000	
Trade debtors	75,000		
provision for doubtful debts	1,708	73,292	
Bank		102,000	295,292
Current liabilities			
Trade creditors		60,000	
Accrued fees		500	60,500
Long-term liabilities			
Farkha		151,410	
Sakhira		100,584	
Sab		75,118	
Nazick		16,680	343,792
Net assets			60,000
Capital			
Farkha		20,000	
Sab		20,000	
Nazick		20,000	60,000

Question 8

Requirement 1

Realisation account

	£		£
Premises	28,500	Capital a/c (Stock) – Nick	11,610
Machinery	16,700	Capital a/c (Premises) – Marshall	38,000
Vehicles	3,640	Capital a/c (Machinery) –	
		Marshall	9,500
Trade debtors	11,950	Capital a/c (Debtors) – Marshall	7,500
Stock	11,000	Capital a/c (Vehicles) – Brendan	2,960
Expenses	679	Capital a/c (Machinery) –	
		Brendan	8,055
		Bank (Remaining trade debtors)	2,300
Profit on realisation			
Marshall	3,728		
Brendan	1,864		
Nick	1,864		
	79,925		79,925

Requirement 2

Bank account

	£		£
Debt agency	2,300	Balance b/d	190
Marshall	8,272	Loan	3,100
		Expenses	679
		Brendan	4,849
		Nick	1,754
	10,572		10,572

Requirement 3

Capital accounts

	Marshall	Brendan	Nick		Marshall	Brendan	Nick
	£	£	£		£	£	£
Stock	–	–	11,610	Bal. b/d	20,000	14,000	11,500
Premises	38,000	–		Trade creditors	4,500	–	–
Machinery	9,500	8,055	–	Mortgage	18,500	–	–
Trade debtors	7,500	–	–	Profit on realisation	3,728	1,864	1,864
Vehicles	–	2,960	–	Bank	8,272	–	–
Bank	–	4,849	1,754				
	55,000	15,864	13,364		55,000	15,864	13,364

Question 9

Requirement 1

Realisation account

	$		$
Vehicles	45,000	Capital (vehicle) – Clyde	10,000
Stock	5,700	Prov. for depreciation	12,200
Debtors	21,800	Prov. for doubtful debts	1,100
Prepayments	290	Bank – vehicles	15,500
Loan interest	250	Bank – stock	6,500
Bank – dissolution expenses	1,500	Bank – trade debtors	17,800
		Bank – prepayments	290
		Trade creditors	4,590
		Bank – goodwill	3,000
		Loss on realisation:	
		Bonnie	1,780
		Clyde	1,780
	74,540		74,540

Requirement 2

Bank

	$		$
Realisation –		Balance b/d	5,000
Vehicles	15,500	Trade creditors	20,900
Stock	6,500	Bank loan	9,250
Debtors	17,800	Realisation – expenses	1,500
Prepayments	290	Accrued expenses	3,000
Goodwill	3,000		
Capital – Clyde	8,780	Capital – Bonnie	12,220
	51,870		51,870

Requirement 3

Capital accounts

	Bonnie	Clyde		Bonnie	Clyde
	$	$		$	$
Current a/c	–	2,000	Bal. b/d	9,000	5,000
Vehicles	–	10,000	Current a/c	5,000	–
Loss on realisation	1,780	1,780			
Bank	12,220	–	Bank	–	8,780
	14,000	13,780		14,000	13,780

Question 10

Requirement 1

Realisation account

	£		£
Premises	65,000	Creditors	13,200
Plant and machinery	49,000	Save the Planet Ltd	190,000
Fixtures and fittings	9,200		
Stock	17,000		
Debtors	21,700		
Profit on realisation:			
Obama	24,780		
Hilary	16,520		
	203,200		203,200

Requirement 2

Bank account

	£		£
Balance b/d	12,300	Capital – Obama	23,770
Save the Planet Ltd	30,000	Capital – Hilary	18,530
	42,300		42,300

Requirement 3

Partners' capital accounts

	Obama	Hilary		Obama	Hilary
	£	£		£	£
Shares in limited			Bal b/d	96,390	56,610
company £160,000 ×			Current a/c	3,400	4,600
(£96,390/153,000),			Profit on realisation	24,780	16,520
£160,000 ×					
(£56,610/153,000)	100,800	59,200			
Cash	23,770	18,530			
	124,570	77,730		124,570	77,730

Requirement 4

Balance sheet as at 1 May 2008

	£	£
Fixed assets		
Premises	90,000	
Plant and machinery	42,000	
Fixtures and fittings	5,500	
Goodwill	33,200	
		170,700
Current assets		
Stock	14,500	
Trade debtors	18,000	
		32,500
Current liabilities		
Trade creditors		13,200
Net assets		190,000
Financed by:		
Share capital		160,000
Share premiums		30,000
		190,000

Chapter 8

General questions

Questions

Question 1

Angelina Jolie opened a business in London on 1 January. She was able to arrange two main agencies under the same business – one for word processing and the other for shoe repairs.

For the first six months, Jolie was able to produce the following information:

Cash receipts	$	$
Initial deposit to start business		5,000
Customers – word processing		6,000
– shoe repairs		3,000
		14,000
Cash payments		
To word processor	4,000	
To shoe repairer	2,500	
Rent	1,000	
Wrappings	500	
Advertising	500	
Motor vehicle	5,000	
Motor vehicle expenses	300	13,800
Cash on hand		200

At the end of December she was able to produce the following additional information:

Completed word processing yet to be paid by customers	500
Completed shoe repairs yet to be paid by customers	100
Amounts owing to word processor	300
Wrappings on hand	200

The advertising payment represents a 12-month advertisement which appears in the shopping centre newspaper.

The motor vehicle was purchased on 1 January and is expected to have a useful life of four years, at which time its residual is expected to be $1,000.

Required
Prepare a profit and loss account for the first six months of Jolie's operations.

Question 2

Prepare a profit and loss account to determine gross and net profit from the following information:

	$		$
Sales	214,000	Sale returns	21,000
Purchases	138,000	Purchase returns	15,000
Electricity	8,320	Carriage Inwards	400
Discounts received	200	Commission received	500
Discounts allowed	110	Wages	28,040
Advertising	200	Rent expense	2,200
Office expenses	670	Insurance	300
Stock 1/7/20x1	38,000	Stock 30/6/20x2	22,500

Use the blank account sheet provided.

	$	$	$
Sales			
Less Sale returns			
Less Cost of goods sold	_____		
Stock (1/7/x1)			
Purchases			
Less Purchase returns			
plus Carriage inwards			
Less Stock (30/6/x2)	_____		
Gross profit		_____	_____
Add other operating income			
Discount received			
Commission received		_____	_____
Less Other operating expenses			
Discount allowed			
Wages			
Electricity			
Advertising			
Rent expense			
Office expenses			
Insurance		_____	_____
Net profit (loss)			══════

Question 3

On 31 May 20x8, the balance sheet of Daponte Trading Ltd appears as follows:

Daponte Trading Ltd
Balance sheet as at 31 May 20x8

Current assets	$	$
Cash	10,000	
Debtors	12,000	
Supplies	6,000	
Stock	25,000	53,000
Fixed assets		
Plant	30,000	
Less Accumulated depreciation	10,000	20,000
Current liabilities		
Creditors		18,000
		55,000
Owner's equity		
Capital		55,000

During the month of June 20x8, Daponte Trading Ltd had the following summary of transactions:

a Received $5,000 from debtors.

b Sold $7,500 worth of stock on credit. This stock had cost $3,000.

c Sold stock costing $5,000 for $12,800 cash.

d Purchased $15,000 stock on credit.

e Paid creditors $14,000.

f Bought supplies for $1,500 cash.

g Paid wages for the month of $3,500.

h Paid rent of $600 for the month.

i Paid annual insurance policy in advance, $840.

j The plant is expected to last for five years with no scrap value. Depreciation adjustment required.

k At end of month had $4,300 of supplies left on hand.

l Adjusted for prepaid insurance used.

Required
From the above information, prepare a profit and loss account and a balance sheet at the end of the month.

Question 4

The following balance sheet is for Ditbit Co. Ltd as at June 2006:

		$	$
Current assets			
Cash		30,000	
Stock		40,000	
Debtors		6,000	76,000
Fixed assets			
Equipment		25,000	
Less Accumulated depreciation		10,000	15,000
			91,000
Current liabilities			
Creditors			25,000
Wages owing			3,000
			28,000
			63,000
Shareholders' funds			
Paid-up capital			60,000
Retained profits			3,000
			63,000

During the following month, just completed, the company had the following transactions:

a Sold stock for cash $30,000 (cost $18,000).

b Sold stock on credit $55,000 (cost 30,000).

c Purchased stock on credit $16,000.

d Paid creditors $24,000.

e Received $18,000 from debtors.

f Issued $10,000 worth of shares at par value, for cash.

g Paid wages of $18,000 which included the wages owing.

h At the end of the month $2,400 was owing in wages.

i The equipment is written off at $500 per month.

j Rent of $2,700 was paid for the quarter beginning 1 July.

Required
From the above information, prepare a profit and loss account and a balance sheet at the end of the month.

Question 5

Below is the trial balance of Mobile Phone Services Ltd, prior to adjustment, and the adjustments which must be made at balance sheet day:

Mobile Phone Services Ltd
Trial balance as at 30 June 20x6

	Debit	Credit
	$	$
Cash	26,400	
Trade debtors	8,400	
Prepaid rent	1,800	
Prepaid insurance	1,100	
Supplies	2,400	
Equipment	42,200	
Trade creditors		6,800
Revenue received		92,600
Loan payable		6,000
Capital – Alesha Dixon		28,000
Drawings – Alesha Dixon	12,000	
Deposits received		2,400
Salaries expense	28,000	
Rent expense	8,400	
Electricity expense	3,400	
Advertising expense	1,700	
	135,800	135,800

The following adjustments are to be made.

a The prepaid rent figure includes $1,200 which relates to the month just completed.

b The prepaid insurance is for a policy which has just expired.

c Since this is the first year of operation and no monthly adjustments have been made, there has been no adjustment made so far for depreciation. All assets have been owned for the full year and it is assessed that the equipment will be usable for ten years. No resale value is assumed.

d Salaries owing at balance date are $1,200.

e Supplies still on hand at balance date cost $800.

f An amount of $1,000 included in the deposits received relates to a contract which has just been completed.

g $800 is receivable from a sub-tenant for rent.

h One month's interest on the bank loan is provided for at 15 percent per annum.

i Five percent of the trade debtors are considered to be doubtful.

Required
Show the adjusting journal entries for Mobile Phone Services Ltd and prepare the profit and loss account and the balance sheet as at 30 June 20x6 for the same company.

Question 6

The transactions below are for a business owned by Mickey Rooney. The business started on 1 July 2009 and has an accounting year-end at 30 June.

July 1 Mickey commenced business by transferring £10,000 to a bank account.
3 Bought fixtures for the shop, £600, paying by cheque.
4 Cash sales, £1,250.
6 Purchased goods on credit from Nice Supplier Ltd to the value of £2,040.
9 Paid £900 by cheque for the first quarter's rent on the premises.
10 Bought goods from Nice Supplier Ltd for cash, £800.
11 Paid an insurance premium by cheque, £80.
14 Paid wages in cash, £350.
15 Sold goods on credit to Nina, £500.
17 Purchased further goods from Nice Supplier Ltd on credit, £1,350.
21 Paid Teal Ltd by cheque the balance on their account.
24 Cash sales, £1,100.
29 Paid wages in cash, £300.
31 Nina settled her account cash.
31 Mickey's business owed to his secretary £50.

Required

1 Do the double-entries and balance the accounts on 31 July.

2 Extract a trial balance as at 31 July 2009 to check the basic accuracy of your work.

Question 7

Cosi, a painter and decorator, has the following transactions during September:

Sept. 1 Cosi started business with £7,000 in cash.
2 Purchases various equipment for £150, pays cash.
3 Purchases ladders for £120, pays cash.
8 Pays £1,000 cash into a business bank account
9 Pays insurance premiums of £100 in cash.
12 Purchases paint and wallpaper for Job. No. 1, for £135, on credit from Paint Ltd.
15 Completes Job. No. 1 and receives £240 cash from customer.
18 Purchases materials for Job. No. 2 for £190 – pays by cheque.
21 Pays secretary's wages, £400 in cash.
24 Purchases second-hand van for £1,900 – pays by cheque.
27 Completes Job. No. 2 for £410. His customer, Mr Aris, has agreed to pay in one month's time.
30 Pays account of WPS Ltd in full, by cheque.

Required

1 Record all transactions in T-accounts.

2 Prepare a profit and loss account for the month.

3 Prepare a balance sheet as at 30 September.

Question 8

The adjusted trial balance of Happy Car Garage Ltd, as at 30 June 2005, appears as follows:

Happy Car Garage Ltd
Adjusted trial balance as at 30 June 2005

	$	$
Cash	36,000	
Trade debtors	4,000	
Supplies	7,000	
Equipment	24,000	
Accumulated depreciation:		
Equipment		3,000
Accrued salaries		3,500
Loan from AZ Finance		19,200
Beyoncy, capital		41,300
Beyoncy, drawings	800	
Service revenue		17,200
Rent expense	1,800	
Supplies expense	1,200	
Salaries expense	6,400	
Depreciation expense	3,000	
	84,200	84,200

George Lexy organised Happy Car Garage Ltd on 2 July 2004 with an initial cash investment of $41,300.

Required

1 Prepare Happy Car Garage Ltd's profit and loss account for the year ended 30 June 2005.

2 Prepare the company's balance sheet as at 30 June.

Question 9

Boat Repairs Services Ltd has the following trial balance as at June 20x1:

	$	$
Cash	4,300	
Trade debtors	9,200	
Prepaid insurance	3,500	
Supplies	1,700	
Plant and equipment	68,700	
Accumulated depreciation:		12,700
Equipment		8,250
Trade creditors		16,500
Loan		64,700
Dell Hewllet, capital	6,700	
Dell Hewllet, drawings		84,500
Service revenue	52,500	
Salaries expense	17,450	
Promotions expense	9,600	
Rent expense	10,600	
Advertising expense	2,400	
	186,650	186,650

Boat Repairs Services Ltd's accountant has identified the following adjustments that must be made:

a A special rain insurance policy costing $800 is still included in the prepaid insurance by error.

b Supplies valued by stocktake $900.

c Depreciation on the equipment for this year is $9,700.

d Five percent of the trade debtors are usually not collected.

e Accrued salaries incurred but not yet paid are $900.

f Interest owing but unpaid on the loan is $200.

Required
Prepare a profit and loss statement and balance sheet. Record the adjusting entries in the general journal.

Question 10

Cutting Tree Services Ltd, which began operations on 1 July 2009, had the following transactions:

July 1 Received €50,000 from Ilias, the owner, as an investment to commence his business.

2 Purchased €15,000 worth of office equipment for cash; the equipment has a life of six years.

3 Paid €960 for a six-month general insurance policy.

8 Received €440 from a client to provide services evenly over the next eight weeks.

11 Paid rent on the premises for the next two months, €4,200.

13 Billed clients for services provided, €6,800.

15 Applied for a loan of €19,000 for the purchase of an office computer.

17 Received €1,750 from clients billed on 14 July.

22 Received the proceeds from the loan that was applied for on the 15 July.

28 Purchased €9,000 worth of the new computer equipment paying for it in cash. This will not be depreciated until the end of next month.

29 Paid the salaries of the office staff, €2,900.

30 Recorded €290 of sundry expenses that were incurred in July but will be paid during the next month.

At 31 July, accrued interest on the loan amounted to €70, while accrued salaries totalled €350. Also, since the last bills were sent out to clients, the firm has provided services billed at €3,400. Three weeks worth of the money received in advance has now been earned.

Required

1 Record the transactions for July in the general journal.

2 Post the journal entries to the correct ledger accounts.

3 Prepare a profit and loss account and balance sheet.

4 Record Cutting Tree Services Ltd's adjusting entries in the journal and post to the correct ledger accounts.

5 Record Cutting Tree Services Ltd's closing entries in the journal and post to the correct ledger accounts.

Question 11

Quick Cleaning Service Ltd rents a shop in Edinburgh. It also does pick-up and delivery for a small fee. It owns two delivery vans and employs three assistants. The balance sheet at 30 June 20x9 was as follows:

Quick Cleaning Service Ltd
Balance sheet as at 30 June 20x9

	£	£
Current assets		
Bank	1,600	
Cleaning materials	950	
Debtors	1,500	4,050
Fixed assets		
Shop fittings	8,550	
Vehicles	15,100	
Equipment	40,100	63,750
Current liabilities		
Creditors		2,870
Non-current liabilities		
Loan – RSS Finance		10,100
Net assets		54,830
Owner's equity		
Capital	50,000	
Add net profit	6,500	
Less Drawings	(1,670)	
		54,830

During the first two weeks in July, the following transactions were recorded on the appropriate documents:

July 1   Takings from customers £150.
    3   Purchased petrol and oil for delivery vans £170.
    4   Purchased cleaning materials £450.
    5   Paid for advertisement in local newspaper £40.
    6   Received £490 from debtors and allowed £30 discount.
        Takings from customers £540.
    8   Paid wages of assistants £350.
    9   Paid creditors £140. Received £5 discount.
    10   Takings from customers £300.
    11   Paid interest on loan £85.
        Paid creditor £520. Received £60 discount.
        Paid for advertisement in local newspaper £40.
    12   Purchased cleaning materials £250.
        Takings from customers £510.
    13   Purchased petrol for delivery vans £70.
    14   Paid wages of assistants £350.
        Purchased shop fittings £380.
        Drawings by owner £500.
        Bank statement received – bank fees £9.
        Cleaning materials on hand at 14 July were valued at £280.

Required

1 Prepare a profit and loss account for the fortnight ending 14 July 20x9.

2 Prepare a balance sheet as at 14 July 20x9.

Use the following blank account sheets.

Requirement 1

Quick Cleaning Service Ltd
Profit and loss account for fortnight ending 14 July 20x9

	£	£
Revenue		
Takings		
Discount received		
Less Expenses		
Petrol and oil		
Advertising		
Discount allowed		
Wages		
Interest expense		
Bank fees		
Cleaning materials used		
Net profit		

Requirement 2

Quick Cleaning Service Ltd
Balance sheet as at 14 July 20x9

	£	£
Current assets		
Cleaning materials		
Debtors		
Fixed assets		
Shop fittings		
Vehicles		
Equipment		
Current liabilities		
Bank		
Creditors		
Long-term liabilities		
Loan – RSS Finance		
Owner's equity		
Capital		

181

Question 12

Data for Jennifer Aniston's business as at 31 December 20x9 are as follows:

	£
Cash at bank	4,000
Fees earned	52,000
Wages	21,000
Trade debtors	7,500
Trade creditors	4,800
Advertising	2,200
Commission earned	17,000
Land and buildings	85,000
Mortgage on land and buildings	45,000
Insurance expense	4,200
Drawings – Jennifer Aniston	8,800
Capital – Jennifer Aniston	?
Stock of stationery	750
Stationery used	250
Discount received	150
Discount allowed	100
Motor vehicles	18,550

Required

1 Prepare a profit and loss account for the year ending 31 December 20x9.

2 Prepare a balance sheet as at 31 December 20x9.

Question 13

Tom Cruise's business has the following balance sheet items on 31 December 20x8:

	£
Bank	(1,200)
Trade debtors	500
Office supplies	1,400
Equipment	15,000
Furniture	400
Motor vehicles	5,200
Trade creditors	730
Bank loan (due December 20x9)	10,000
Capital – Tom Cruise	?

During the first two weeks of January 20x9, the following transactions occurred:

January	1	Cruise contributed additional capital of £2,000 in cash and furniture worth £500.
	3	Paid creditors amount owing.
		Billed customers for services performed £7,000.
	4	Purchased equipment worth £1,000 on credit.

6 Paid the following week's expenses:
   Wages   £800
   Rent   £500
   Petrol   £300
7 Cruise withdrew £80 for his personal use.
9 Billed customers for services performed £3,800.
   Reduced bank loan by £2,000.
   Received £4,500 from debtors.
11 Purchased office supplies £600.
13 Office supplies used for the period £850.
   Paid the following week's expenses:
   Wages   £750
   Rent   £500
   Petrol   £400

Required

1 Prepare a profit and loss account for the first two weeks of January 20x9.

2 Prepare a balance sheet as at 14 January 20x9.

Question 14

Theo Paphetes, a retailer of office equipment and stationery, works from home and started his business on 1 March with £450,000 capital in cash. During the month of March, the following transactions take place:

Mar. 1 Buys desk for his office at home, £500, pays cash.
2 Purchases stationery from Stationery Suppliers Ltd. for £65,000, on credit.
3 Buys delivery van for £2,100, on six month's credit, from Garage Ltd.
7 Purchases further stationery from Stationery Suppliers Ltd for £10,000, on credit.
9 Cash sales of stationery £51,000.
10 Purchases office equipment (for resale) £15,000, on credit from Stationery Suppliers Ltd.
12 Cash sales of stationery £22,000.
15 Borrows £20,000 from his uncle and deposits the amount in the business's bank current account, as the whole of this amount is to be used in Theos' business. The loan must be repaid within the next 12 months.
18 Sells office equipment to James Caane for £3,000 on credit.
21 Rents a warehouse and pays £500 rent (for the month of March) by cheque.
22 Pays secretary's wages in cash, £800.
24 Pays £40,000 cheque to Stationery Suppliers Ltd in part settlement of account.
27 Pays for service of van, insurance, and tax amounting to £900, by cheque.
28 Cash sales of stationery, £15,000.
29 Sells all remaining stock of stationery and equipment for £12,000, cash.
31 Pays £500,000 cash into the business bank account.

Required

1 Record all transactions in T-accounts.

2 Prepare a profit and loss account for the month.

3 Prepare a balance sheet as at 31 March 20x6.

Question 15

Stars Ltd's account balances at 31 December 20x5 are as follows:

	£		£
Bank overdraft	1,620	Cash on hand	400
Debtors	4,000	Creditors	5,000
Cash sales	54,000	Cash purchases	42,000
Credit purchases	9,000	Credit sales	26,000
Sales returns	950	Purchase returns	1,100
Stock (1/1/20x5)	6,500	Stock (31/12/20x5)	5,400
Electricity	350	Office equipment	6,900
Office furniture	1,200	Motor vehicles	28,000
Bank loan	17,000	Rent expense	9,800
Advertising	3,000	Wages	5,600
Office expenses	1,300	Carriage inwards	850
Carriage outwards	1,280	Discount received	380
Discount allowed	1,000	Sundry expenses	870
Stationery	450	Capital	18,350
Drawings	1,250	Commission received	1,250

Required

1 Prepare a profit and loss statement for the year ending 31 December 20x5.

2 Prepare a classified balance sheet as at 31 December 20x5.

Question 16

Phototronic Services Ltd has employed you as its accountant to record its business transactions. On 1 September 20x8, the following balance sheet is presented:

Phototronic Services Ltd
Balance sheet as at 1 September 20x8

	£	£
Current assets		
Trade debtors	9,000	
Stock	15,000	24,000
Fixed assets		
Land	25,000	
Warehouse	20,000	
Motor vehicles	18,000	63,000
Current liabilities		
Bank overdraft	2,100	
Trade creditors	7,200	9,300
Net assets		77,700
Owner's equity		
Capital – Matt Damon	68,000	
Plus profit	17,000	
Less drawings	7,300	77,700

Additional information:

Sept. 3 Sold goods on credit to Russell Crowe £300.
Received from George Clooney £2,940 cash, and a discount allowed £60.
Purchased goods on credit from Hilary Duff £480.

6 Damon deposited £24,000 in the business's bank account.
Purchased stationery £60.

7 Sales on credit to Denzel Washington £990.
Cash sales £180.

8 Sales on credit to George Clooney £2,880.
Received from Nicole Kidman £1,764 cash, and a discount allowed £36.

9 Paid for petrol and oil £60.

10 Purchased goods on credit from Jessica Biel £1,800.
Credit sales to Nicole Kidman £1,320.
Sales on credit to Denzel Washington £1,650.

11 Purchased stamps £78 for cash.
Paid fire insurance £288.

13 Credit sales to Johnny Depp £2,520.
Cash sales £510.

14 Paid Hilary Duff £1,470, discount allowed £30.
Purchased office supplies £95 cash.

15 Purchase on credit from Lindsay Lohan £1,200.

16 Sales on credit to Johnny Depp £2,400.

18 Johnny Depp returns goods worth £60.

21 Received from Will Smith £2,646 cash and a discount allowed £54.

23 Return to Lindsay Lohan goods (purchased on 15 September) worth £240.

25 Received from Russell Crowe £1,500 cash.
Cash sales £132.

28 Purchased stamps £78 for cash.
Paid for petrol and oil £72.

30 Purchased two new computers £720.

Additional information at 30 September 20x8:

a Stock on hand £11,000.

b Monthly wages owing £2,100.

c The fire insurance is a 12-month premium expiring 31/08/20x9.

d Phototronic Services Ltd has earned commission of £2,450 for September. Payment is expected to be received in October.

e Depreciation on the vehicles for September is £150.

f Stationery on hand £25.

g Office supplies on hand £35.

Required

1 Produce the general journal incorporating all the above information.

2 Post all the above transactions to the general ledger.

3 Produce a profit and loss account for the month September 20x8.

4 Produce a balance as at 30 September 20x8.

Question 17

Below is the trial balance on 31 December 2008 of a sole trader's business, prior to adjustment, and the adjustments which must be made at balance sheet day:

	Dr £	Cr £
Fixtures and fittings (cost)	1,500	
Provision for depreciation of fixtures and fittings		800
Stock	1,800	
Purchases	7,500	
Discounts allowed	350	
Rent and rates	670	
Cash	120	
Sales		12,940
Returns inwards	200	
Returns outwards		90
Trade debtors and trade creditors	4,300	3,300
Wages and salaries	3,250	
General expenses	330	
Motor vehicles (cost)	3,000	
Provision for depreciation of motor vehicles		2,250
Discounts received		200
Bank		940
Capital		2,500
	23,020	23,020

Additional information:

a Stock on 31 December 2008, valued at £2,000.

b Depreciation is to be provided for as follows:

Motor vehicles – 25 percent of cost (straight line method)

Fixtures and fittings – 10 percent of reduced balance.

c General expenses owing at 31 December 2008, £50.

d Rates prepaid at 31 December 2008, £20.

e Wages and salaries accrued at 31 December 2008, £100.

Required

1 Prepare the profit and loss account for the year ended 31 December 2008.

2 Prepare the balance sheet at that date.

Question 18

The following trial balance was extracted from the books of a sole trader, as at 31 December 2006:

	£	£
Trade creditors		7,555
Sales		72,500
Furniture and fittings	1,000	
Motor vans	1,610	
Stock	5,100	
Discounts received		1,367
Trade debtors	4,980	
General expenses	1,888	
Purchases	52,587	
Motor expenses	1,100	
Equipment	4,510	
Rent and rates	421	
Discounts allowed	875	
Wages and salaries	9,800	
Bank	8,451	
Capital account		11,400
Lighting and heating	500	
	92,822	92,822

At the end of December the trader was able to produce the following additional information:

a Stock on 31 December 2006 is £9,687.

b Lighting and heating of £60 accrued on 31 December 2006.

c Rates of £67 paid in advance on 31 December 2006.

d The motor vans account appeared in the books as follows:

Motor vans

2006		£	2006		£
1 Jan.	Balance b/d (old van)	354	1 Jan.	Cash – sale of old van	244
	Cash – cost of new van	1,500	31 Dec.	Balance c/d	1,610
		1,854			1,854
2007					
1 Jan.	Balance b/d	1,610			

Note: the balance b/d of £354 on 1 January 2006 is the net book value of the old van. Depreciation on the new van is at the rate of 20 percent per annum. Ignore depreciation of furniture and fittings and equipment.

Required

1 Prepare the profit and loss account for the year ended 31 December 2006.

2 Prepare the balance sheet as at 31 December.

Question 19

The following trial balance was extracted from the books of a sole trader, as at 31 December 2008:

	£	£
Sales		65,000
Repairs to buildings	3,500	
Car expenses	440	
Provision for doubtful debts		170
Freehold land and buildings	10,000	
Furniture and fittings	1,500	
Purchases	48,000	
Wages and salaries	8,606	
Rates and insurances	348	
Discounts allowed	1,199	
Motor car	1,850	
Discounts received		1,040
Drawings	2,500	
Bad debts	390	
Trade debtors	4,987	
General expenses	1,680	
Trade creditors		5,310
Bank	1,420	
Capital account		21,000
Opening stock	6,100	
	92,520	92,520

At the end of December the trader was able to produce the following additional information:

a Stock on 31 December 2008 is £9,200.

b During 2008 the sole trader withdrew goods valued at £5,000 for his own private use.

c Rates and insurances paid in advance at 31 December 2008, is £48.

d Wages and salaries outstanding at 31 December 2008 is £494.

e The provision for doubtful debts is to be reduced to £90.

f One fourth of the car expenses represents the costs of the sole trader's motoring for private, as distinct from business, purposes.

g The item 'Repairs to buildings £3,500' includes £2,500 in respect of alterations and improvements to the buildings.

Required

1 Prepare the profit and loss account for the year ended 31 December 2008, and

2 Prepare the balance sheet at that date.

Note: ignore depreciation of fixed assets.

Question 20

Alex Boots, a retailer, has produced the following information:

a Summary of the bank account for the year ended 30 April 2009.

	£		£
Balance 1 May 2008	1,890	Purchases of goods for resale	25,542
Receipts from sales	33,521	Alex's personal drawings	7,200
		Redecoration of Alex's private house	844
		Additional fixtures and fittings purchased 1 November, 2008	140
		Payments for general expenses	985
		Balance 30 April 2009	700
	35,411		35,411

b Assets and liabilities, other than balance at bank:

Additional information at 30 April:	2008	2009
	£	£
Fixtures and fittings (at cost less depreciation)	1,260	?
Motor vehicle (at cost less depreciation)	900	?
Trade debtors	985	850
Trading stock	7,450	6,780
Trade creditors	1,200	1,150

c It is Alex Boots' policy to provide depreciation on fixtures and fittings at 10 percent per annum and on the motor vehicle at 25 percent per annum, both on the reducing balance method.

d Alex Boots withdrew £420 (at cost) of the stock for his own consumption.

Required

1 Prepare Alex's profit and loss account for the year ended 30 April 2009.

2 Prepare Alex's balance sheet as at 30 April 2009.

Question 21

On 1 January 2006, a business's list of assets and liabilities are as follows:

	£		£
Mortgage loan	50,000	Premises	80,000
Rates in advance	450	Stock	3,820
Trade creditors	2,810	Bank	6,555
Motor vehicles	11,100		

The business's sales are strictly for cash only. The owner of the business does not keep any books at all.

During the financial year, the following transactions took place:

	£
Cash paid into bank, proceeds of cash sales	98,234
Cheques drawn for payments to suppliers	45,279
Cash discount deducted (received)	621
Cheques drawn for expense items	2,250
Cheques drawn for private expenditure	16,400

During the year rates amounting to £2,000 had been paid (by cheque) for the period 1 April 2006 to 31 March 2007.

Repayments of the mortgage loan have been made by standing order at the bank at the rate of £300 per calendar month, but the account has been debited with £600 interest by the mortgage holder.

On 31 December 2006 the following balances were provided:

	£
Stock	4,590
Motor vehicles	10,000
Trade creditors	3,680

Required

1 Prepare the profit and loss account for the year ended 31 December 2006.

2 Prepare the balance sheet as at 31 December 2006.

Answers

Question 1

Requirement 1

Profit and loss account for the first six months of operations

	$	$
Revenue		
Word processing	6,500	
Shoe repairs	3,100	9,600
Less Expenses		
Word processor	4,300	
Shoe repairer	2,500	
Rent	1,000	
Wrappings	300	
Advertising	250	
Motor vehicle expenses	300	
Depreciation of motor vehicle	500	9,150
Net profit (loss)		(450)

Question 2

No solution is given for this question, students should attempt to answer it themselves.

Question 3

Requirement 1

Daponte Trading Ltd
Profit and loss account for June 20x8

	$	$
Revenue		
Credit sales	7,500	
Cash sales	12,800	20,300
Less Cost of sales		8,000
		12,300
Less Expenses		
Wages	3,500	
Rent	600	
Depreciation	500	
Supplies	3,200	
Insurance	70	
Total *expenses*		7,870
Operating profit		4,430

Requirement 2

Daponte Trading Ltd
Balance sheet as at 30 June 20x8

	$	$
Current assets		
Cash	7,360	
Debtors	14,500	
Supplies	4,300	
Stock	32,000	
Prepayments	770	58,930
Fixed assets		
Plant	30,000	
Less Accumulated depreciation	10,500	19,500
Current liabilities		
Creditors		19,000
		59,430
Owner's equity		
Capital		55,000
Profit		4,430
		59,430

Question 4

No solution is given for this question. Students should attempt to answer it themselves.

Question 5

No solution is given for this question. Students should attempt to answer it themselves.

Question 6

Requirement 1

Capital

		£			£
31 Jul.	Balance c/d	10,000	1 Jul.	Bank	10,000

Bank

		£			£
1 Jul.	Capital	10,000	3 Jul.	Fixtures	600
			9 Jul.	Rent	900
			11 Jul.	Insurance	80
			21 Jul.	Nice Supplier	3,390
			31 Jul.	Balance c/d	5,030
		10,000			10,000

Fixtures

		£			£
3 Jul.	Bank	600	31 Jul.	Balance c/d	600

Cash

		£			£
4 Jul.	Sales	1,250	10 Jul.	Purchases	800
24 Jul.	Sales	1,100	14 Jul.	Wages	350
31 Jul.	Nina	500	29 Jul.	Wages	300
			30 Jul.	Balance c/d	1,400
		2,850			2,850

Trade Creditor – Nice Supplier Ltd

		£			£
21 Jul.	Bank	3,390	6 Jul.	Purchases	2,040
			17 Jul.	Purchases	1,350
		3,390			3,390

Trade debtor – Nina

		£			£
15 Jul.	Sales	500	31 Jul.	Cash	500

Purchases

		£			£
6 Jul.	Nice Supplier	2,040	31 Jul.	Balance c/d	4,190
10 Jul.	Nice Supplier	800			
21 Jul.	Teal	1,350			
		4,190			4,190

Sales

		£			£
31 Jul.	Balance c/d	2,850	4 Jul.	Cash	1,250
			15 Jul.	Nina	500
			24 Jul.	Cash	1,100
		2,850			2,850

Rent

		£			£
9 Jul.	Bank	900	31 Jul.	Balance c/d	300
			31 Jul.	Prepayment	600
		900			900

Wages

		£			£
14 Jul.	Cash	350	31 Jul.	Balance c/d	700
29 Jul.	Cash	300			
31 Jul.	Accrual	50			
		700			700

Prepaid Rent

		£			£
31 Jul.	Rent	600	31 Jul.	Balance c/d	600

Insurance

		£			£
11 Jul.	Bank	80	31 Jul.		80

Accrued wages

		£			£
31 Jul.	Balance c/d	50	31 Jul.	Wages	50

Requirement 2

Trial balance as at 31 July

	Dr	Cr
	£	£
Capital		10,000
Bank	5,030	
Fixtures	600	
Cash	1,400	
Nice Supplier Ltd		0
Nina	0	
Purchases	4,190	
Sales		2,850
Rent	300	
Wages	700	
Prepaid rent	600	
Insurance	80	
Accrued wages		50
	12,900	12,900

Question 7

Requirement 1

Capital

		£			£
30 Sep.	Balance c/d	7,000	1 Sep.	Cash	7,000
			1 Oct.	Balance b/d	7,000

Cash

		£			£
1 Sep.	Capital	7,000	2 Sep.	Equipment	150
15 Sep.	Sales	240	3 Sep.	Equipment	120
			9 Sep.	Insurance	100
			8 Sep.	Bank	1,000
			21 Sep.	Wages	400
			30 Sep.	Balance c/d	5,470
		7,240			7,240
1 Oct.	Balance b/d	5,470			

Equipment

		£			£
2 Sep.	Cash	150	30 Sep.	Balance c/d	270
3 Sep.	Cash	120			
		270			270
1 Oct.	Balance b/d	270			

Bank

		£			£
8 Sep.	Cash	1,000	18 Sep.	Purchases	190
			24 Sep.	Motor vehicle – van	1,900
30 Sep.	Balance c/d	1,225	29 Sep.	Paint Ltd	135
		2,225			2,225
			1 Oct.	Balance b/d	1,225

Trade creditor – Paint Ltd

		£			£
30 Sep.	Bank	135	12 Sep.	Purchases	135

Trade debtor – Mr Aris

		£			£
27 Sep.	Sales	410	30 Sep.	Balance b/d	410
1 Oct.	Balance b/d	410			

Motor vehicles – van

		£			£
24 Sep.	Bank	1,900	30 Sep.	Balance b/d	1,900
1 Oct.	Balance b/d	1,900			

Insurance

		£			£
9 Sep.	Cash	100	30 Sep.	P&L a/c	100
		100			100

Purchases

		£			£
12 Sep.	Paint Ltd	135	30 Sep.	P&L a/c	325
18 Sep.	Bank	190			
		325			325

Wages

		£			£
21 Sep.	Cash	400	30 Sep.	P&L a/c	400
		400			400

Sales

		£			£
30 Sep.	P&L a/c	650	15 Sep.	Cash	240
			27 Sep.	Mr Aris	410
		650			650

Requirement 2

Profit and loss account for month of September

		£
Sales		650
Purchases		325
Gross profit		325
Expenses:		
Insurances	100	
Wages	400	500
Net loss		(175)

Requirement 3

Balance sheet as at 30 September

	£	£
Fixed assets		
Equipment	270	
Motor vans	1,900	2,170
Current assets		
Debtors	410	
Cash	5,470	5,880
Current liabilities		
Bank	1,225	1,225
		6,825
Capital		7,000
Loss for the year		(175)
		6,825

Question 8

No solution is given for this question. Students should attempt to answer it themselves.

Question 9

No solution is given for this question. Students should attempt to answer it themselves.

Question 10

No solution is given for this question. Students should attempt to answer it themselves.

Question 11

No solution is given for this question. Students should attempt to answer it themselves.

Question 12

Requirement 1

Jennifer Aniston's business
Profit and loss account for the year ending 31 December 20x9

	£	£
Revenue		
Fees earned	52,000	
Commission earned	17,000	
Discount received	150	69,150
Less Expenses		
Wages	21,000	
Advertising	2,200	
Insurance	4,200	
Stationery used	250	
Discount allowed	100	27,750
Net profit		$41,400

Requirement 2

Jennifer Aniston's business
Balance sheet as at 31 December 20x9

		$	$
Current assets			
Cash at bank		4,000	
Trade debtors		7,500	
Stock of stationery		750	12,250
Fixed assets			
Land and buildings		85,000	
Motor vehicles		18,550	103,550
Current liabilities			
Trade creditors			4,800
Long-term liabilities			
Mortgage on land and buildings			45,000
Net assets			66,000
Owner's equity			
Capital – 1 January 20x9	(2)		33,400
Net profit for year			41,400
Less Drawings			(8,800)
Capital – 31 December 20x9	(1)		66,000

(1) From net assets.

(2) Working back from (1).

Question 13

Requirement 1

TOM CRUISE'S BUSINESS
Profit and loss account for the fortnight ending 14 January 20x9

	£	£
Revenue		
Fees		10,800
Less Expenses		
Wages	1,550	
Rent	1,000	
Petrol	700	
Office supplies used	850	4,100
Net profit		6,700

Requirement 2

TOM CRUISE'S BUSINESS
Balance sheet as at 14 January 20x9

	£	£
Current assets		
Trade debtors	6,800	
Stock of office supplies	1,150	7,950
Fixed assets		
Equipment	16,000	
Furniture	900	
Motor vehicle	5,200	22,100
Current liabilities		
Bank overdraft	1,360	
Trade creditors	1,000	
Bank loan	8,000	10,360
Net assets		19,690
Owner's equity		
Capital – 31 December 20x8	10,570	
Plus Net profit	6,700	
Plus Additional capital	2,500	
Less drawings	80	
Capital – 14 January 20x9		19,690

Question 14

See the accompanying website for the answers.

Question 15

See the accompanying website for the answers.

Question 16

Requirement 1

General journal

Phototronic Services Ltd

Date	Description	Debit	Credit
20x8 Sept. 3	Trade debtors	300	
	Sales		300
	Bank	2,940	
	Discount allowed	60	
	Trade debtors		3,000
	Purchases	480	
	Trade creditors		480
6	Bank	24,000	
	Capital – Kimgar		24,000
	Stationery	60	
	Bank		60
7	Trade debtors	990	
	Sales		990
	Bank	180	
	Sales		180
8	Trade debtors	2,880	
	Sales		2,880
	Bank	1,764	
	Discount allowed	36	
	Trade debtors		1,800
9	Petrol and oil	60	
	Bank		60
10	Purchases	1,800	
	Trade creditors		1,800
	Trade debtors	1,320	
	Sales		1,320
	Trade debtors	1,650	
	Sales		1,650

Date	Description	Debit	Credit
11	Postage Bank	78	78
	Insurance Bank	288	288
13	Trade debtors Sales	2,520	2,520
	Bank Sales	510	510
14	Trade creditors Bank Discount received	1,500	1,470 30
	Office supplies Bank	95	95
15	Purchases Trade creditors	1,200	1,200
16	Trade debtors Sales	2,400	2,400
18	Sales returns Trade debtors	60	60
21	Bank Discount Allowed Trade debtors	2,646 54	2,700
23	Trade creditors Purchase returns	240	240
25	Bank Trade debtors	1,500	1,500
	Bank Sales	132	132
28	Postage Bank	78	78
	Petrol and oil Bank	72	72
30	Office equipment Bank	720	720

Requirement 2

Phototronic Services Ltd
General ledger

Bank

1/9		2,940	1/9	Bal	2,100
6/9		24,000	6/9		60
7/9		180	9/9		60
8/9		1,764	11/9		78
13/9		510	11/9		288
21/9		2,646	14/9		1,470
25/9		1,500	14/9		95
25/9		132	28/9		78
			28/9		72
			30/9		720
			30/9		28,651

Trade debtors

1/9	Bal	9,000	1/9	3,000
1/9		300	8/9	1,800
7/9		990	18/9	60
8/9		2,880	21/9	2,700
10/9		1,320	25/9	1,500
10/9		1,650		
13/9		2,520		
16/9		2,400		
			30/9	12,000

Land

1/9	Bal	25,000

Stock

1/9	Bal	15,000

Vehicles

1/9	Bal	18,000

Warehouse

1/9	Bal	20,000

Office equipment

30/9	720

Trade creditors

14/9	1,500	1/9	Bal	7,200
23/9	240	1/9		480
		10/9		1,800
		15/9		1,200
30/9	8,940			

Capital – Matt Damon

		1/9	Bal	77,700
		6/9		24,000
30/9	101,700			

Sales

	1/9	300
	7/9	990
	7/9	180
	8/9	2,880
	10/9	1,320
	10/9	1,650
	13/9	2,520
	13/9	510
	16/9	2,400
	25/9	132
30/9	12,882	

Sales returns and allowances

18/9	60

Purchases

1/9	480
10/9	1,800
15/9	1,200
30/9	3,480

Purchase returns and allowances

23/9	240

Discount allowed				Discount received		
1/9	60				14/9	30
8/9	36					
21/9	54					
		30/9	150			

Stationery			Petrol and oil			
6/9	60		9/9	60		
			28/9	72		
					30/9	132

Postage				Insurance		
11/9	78			11/9	288	
28/9	78					
		30/9	156			

Office supplies		
14/9	95	

Requirement 3

Phototronic Services Ltd
Profit and loss account for September 20x8

	£	£	£
Revenue			
Sales		12,882	
Less sale returns and allowances		60	12,822
Less Cost of goods sold			
Stock (1/9/20x8)		15,000	
Purchases	3,480		
Less purchase returns	240	3,240	
Less stock (30/9/20x8)		11,000	7,240
Gross profit			5,582
Add other operating revenue			
Discount received		30	
Commission received		2,450	2,480
			8,062
Less Other operating expenses			
Discount allowed		150	
Stationery		35	
Petrol and oil		132	
Postage		156	
Insurance		24	
Office supplies		60	
Wages		2,100	
Depreciation of vehicles		150	2,807
Net profit			5,255

Requirement 4

Phototronic Services Ltd

Balance sheet as at 30 September 20x8

	£	£	£
Current assets			
Bank		28,651	
Trade debtors		12,000	
Stock		11,000	
Prepaid expenses		264	
Commission receivable		2,450	
Stock of stationery		25	
Stock of office supplies		35	54,425
Fixed assets			
Land		25,000	
Warehouse		20,000	
Vehicles	18,000		
Less acc. depreciation	150	17,850	
Office equipment		720	63,570
Current liabilities			
Trade creditors		8,940	
Accrued expenses		2,100	11,040
Net assets			106,955
Owner's equity			
Capital – Matt Damon		101,700	
Plus Net profit		5,255	106,955

Question 17

Requirement 1

Profit and loss account for year ended 31 December 2008

	£	£	£
Sales		12,940	
Less Returns inwards		200	12,740
Cost of goods sold			
Stock		1,800	
Purchases	7,500		
Less Returns outwards	90	7,410	
Less Stock		2,000	7,210
Gross profit			5,530
Discounts received			200
Expenses:			
Discounts allowed		350	
Rent and rates		650	
Wages and salaries		3,350	
General expenses		380	
Depreciation on:			
Motor vehicles		750	
Fixtures and fittings		70	5,550
Net profit			180

Requirement 2

Balance sheet as at 31 December 2008

Fixed assets		
Motor vehicles (cost)	3,000	
Less provision for depreciation	3,000	0
Fixtures and fittings (cost)	1,500	
Less Provision for depreciation	870	630
Current assets		
Stock	2,000	
Debtors	4,300	
Cash	120	
Rates prepaid	20	6,440
Current liabilities		
Creditors	3,300	
Wages accrued	100	
General expenses acrued	50	
Bank overdraft	940	4,390
Net assets		2,680
Capital		2,500
Profit for the year		180
		2,680

Question 18

Requirement 1

Profit and loss account for year ended 31 December 2006

	£	£
Sales		72,500
Cost of goods sold		
Stock	5,100	
Purchases	52,587	
Less Stock	9,687	48,000
Gross profit		24,500
Discount received		1,367
Expenses:		
General expenses	1,888	
Motor expenses	1,100	
Rent and rates	354	
Discounts allowed	875	
Wages and salaries	9,800	
Light and heat	560	
Loss on sale of van	110	
Depreciation of vans	300	14,987
		10,880

Requirement 2

Balance sheet as at 31 December 2006

	£	£
Fixed assets		
Motor vehicles (cost)	1,500	
Less Provision for depreciation	300	1,200
Furniture and fittings		1,000
Equipment		4,510
Current assets		
Stock	9,687	
Trade debtors	4,980	
Bank	8,451	
Rates prepaid	67	23,185
Current liabilities		
Trade creditors	7,555	
Light and heat accrued	60	7,615
Net assets		22,280
Capital		11,400
Profit for the year		10,880
		22,280

Question 19

Requirement 1

Profit and loss account for year ended 31 December 2008

	£	£
Sales		65,000
Cost of goods sold		
Stock	6,100	
Purchases	48,000	
Less Stock	9,200	44,900
Gross profit		20,100
Discount received		1,040
Provision for doubtful debts		80
Expenses:		
Repairs to buildings	1,000	
Car expenses	330	
Wages and salaries	9,100	
Rates and insurance	300	
Discounts allowed	1,199	
Bad debts	390	
General expenses	1,680	13,999
Net profit		7,221

Requirement 2

Balance sheet as at 31 December 2008

	£	£	£
Fixed assets			
Freehold land and buildings		10,000	
Plus Additions		2,500	7,500
Furniture and fittings			1,500
Motor car			1,850
Current assets			
Stock		9,200	
Trade debtors	4,987		
Less Provision for doubtful debts	90	4,897	
Rates and insurance prepaid		48	
Bank		1,420	15,565
Current liabilities			
Trade creditors		5,310	
Wages and salaries accrued		494	5,804
			20,611
Capital			21,000
Plus Net profit			7,221
Less Drawings (2,500 + 5,000 + 110)			7,610
			20,611

Question 20

Requirement 1

Alex Boots
Profit and loss account for the year ended 30 April 2009

	£	£
Sales		33,386
Less Cost of sales		
Stock at 1 May 2008	7,450	
Plus Purchases (25,492 – 420)	25,072	
	75,890	
Less Stock at 30 April 2009	6,780	25,742
Gross profit		7,644
Less Expenditure		
General expenses	985	
Depreciation on:		
Fixtures and fittings (126 + 14)	140	
Motor van	225	1,350
Net profit		6,294

Requirement 2

Alex Boots
Balance sheet as at 30 April 2009

	£	£
Fixed assets		
Fixtures and fittings (NBV)		1,260
Motor vehicle (NBV)		675
		1,935
Current assets		
Stock	6,780	
Trade debtors	850	
Bank	700	8,330
Less Current liabilities		
Trade creditors	1,150	1,150
Net assets		9,115
Capital		
Balance at 1 May 2008		11,285
Plus Profit for year		6,294
		17,579
Less Drawings (7,200 + 420 + 844)		8,464
Balance at 30 April 2009		9,115

Question 21

Requirement 1

Profit and loss account for the year ended 31 December 2006

	£	£
Sales		98,234
Less Cost of sales		
Stock at 1 January 2006	3,820	
Add Purchases	46,770	
	75,890	
Less Stock at 31 December 2006	4,590	46,000
Gross profit		52,234
Discounts received		621
Less Expenditure		
Expenses	2,250	
Rates	1,950	
Interest	600	
Depreciation of van	1,100	5,900
Net profit		46,955

Requirement 2

Balance sheet as at 31 December 2006

	£	£
Fixed assets		
Premises		80,000
Motor vehicles (NBV)		10,000
		90,000
Current assets		
Stock	4,590	
Rates in advance	500	
Bank	35,260	40,350
Less Current liabilities		
Mortgage loan	47,000	
Trade creditors	3,680	50,680
Net assets		79,670
Capital		
Balance at 1 January 2006		49,115
Plus Profit for year		46,955
		96,070
Less Drawings		16,400
Balance at 31 December 2006		79,670

Glossary

Account: a record of business transactions, part of double entry records, containing details of transactions for each specific financial statement item.

Account payable (or **trade payable,** or **trade creditor**): a business or person to whom money is owed for goods purchased or services rendered, or, differently, a liability owed to suppliers for goods purchased or services rendered.

Account receivable (or **trade debtor**): a business or person who owes money to another business for goods or services supplied, or, differently, amounts owed to a business (after selling on credit) whether or not they are currently due.

Accounting: the process of designing and operating an information system for collecting, measuring and recording business transactions (activities), and summarising and communicating the results of these transactions to users to facilitate making informed judgements and financial/economic decisions.

Accounts (or **final accounts,** or **financial statements**): a term previously used to refer to financial statements produced at the end of an accounting period, such as the profit and loss account (or income statement), the balance sheet and the cashflow statement. Nowadays, the term 'financial statements' is more commonly used.

Accrual (or simply **accrued expense**): an expense that is incurred, for which the benefit has been received but which has not yet been paid for by the end of the accounting period. It is included in the relevant expense account and in the balance sheet under current liabilities as 'accruals' or 'accrued expense'.

Accrued expense (or simply **accrual**): an expense that is incurred, for which the benefit has been received but which has not yet been paid for by the end of the accounting period. It is included in the relevant expense account and in the balance sheet under current liabilities as 'accrued expense' or 'accruals'.

Accrued income: income (normally) from a source other than the main source of business income, such as rent receivable, that was due to be received by the end of the period but which has not been received by that date, so it is expected to be received in a subsequent period. It is added to the relevant income account and to accounts receivable under the current assets in the balance sheet.

Accumulated depreciation (or **provision for depreciation account**): the account where depreciation of fixed assets is accumulated for balance sheet purposes. The accumulated depreciation is subtracted from the original cost or valuation of the asset to arrive at its net book value in the balance. The accumulated depreciation amount represents only the expired value of an asset; it is neither cash nor any other type of asset that can be used to purchase another asset.

Allowance for doubtful debts (or **provision for doubtful debts**): an account representing an estimate of the expected amount of trade debtors (i.e. debts to business) at the balance sheet date which may not pay (i.e. be irrecoverable).

Amortisation: a term used instead of 'depreciation' for the intangible assets.

Assets: resources owned by a business.

Bad debt: a trade debtor who is unlikely to be able to pay, or a debt that a business will not be able to collect.

Bad debt expense: an expense that is associated with a business's inability to collect the amount owed to that business by its trade debtor.

Balance brought down: the opening balance of a new accounting period, transferred from the previous accounting period. It is the difference between both sides of a T-account that is entered below the totals on the opposite side to the one on which the balance carried down was entered. (This is normally abbreviated to 'balance b/d'.)

Balance carried down: the closing balance of a T-account at the end of an accounting period and the amount that will become the opening balance for the next accounting period. It is the difference between both sides of an account that is entered above the totals and makes the total of both sides equal each other. (This is normally abbreviated to 'balance c/d'.)

Balance off the T-account: insert the difference (called a 'balance') between the two sides of an account and then total and rule off the account. This is normally done at the end of a period (usually a month, a quarter or a year).

Balance sheet: a statement showing the financial position of a business on a specified date (i.e. the business's assets, liabilities and capital). It is a list of the physical resources (assets) owned by a business at a particular date, shown at the proportion of their original cost which remains unused (unexpired cost), net of amounts owed by the business (liabilities).

Bank loan: an amount of money advanced by a bank that has a fixed rate of interest that is charged on the full amount and is repayable on a specified future date.

Bookkeeping: the process of systematic recording of financial aspects of a business's transactions and activities in the appropriate accounting books.

Capital: the total of resources (cash and other assets) invested and left in a business by its owner(s). It can also be seen as the amount the business owes back to its owners.

Capital expenditure: any asset-related expenditures with benefits extending beyond the current year, or when a business spends money to buy or add value to a fixed asset.

Carriage inwards: transport or delivery expenses incurred through the purchase of goods from suppliers (trade creditors) of a business. It is added to the purchases figure in the profit and loss account, as it is part of the cost of the goods being purchased.

Carriage outwards: transport or delivery expenses incurred through the sale of goods to customers (trade debtors) of a business. It is taken up as an expense in the profit and loss account.

Cash: ready money, including cash balances and bank balances, customer cheques, and plus funds invested in 'cash equivalents'.

Close off the account: totalling and ruling off an account on which there is no outstanding balance.

Credit: the right-hand side of the accounts in double entry. It has the effect of increasing a capital, liability or revenue (income) account, and decreasing an asset or expense account.

Current assets: assets consisting of cash, bank, goods for resale (stock), trade debtors or other items having a short life: they are constantly flowing in and out of a business in the normal course of a business. In accounting, any asset expected to last or be in use for less than one year is considered a current asset.

Current liabilities: liabilities (obligations) such as trade creditors, accruals and unpaid taxes, arising in the normal course of a business and which must be paid within a year of the balance sheet date.

Debit: the left-hand side of the accounts in double entry. It has the effect of increasing an asset or expense account, and decreasing a capital, liability or revenue (income) account.

Depletion: a term used instead of 'depreciation' for the natural resources.

Depreciation: a system of cost allocation. The part of the cost of a fixed asset consumed during its period of use by the business. It represents an estimate of how much of the overall economic usefulness of a fixed asset has been used up in each accounting period and, as a result, it reflects reduction in the net book value of the asset due to usage and/or obsolescence. It is charged as a debit to profit and loss, and a credit against fixed asset accounts in the general ledger.

Discounts allowed: an expense in the profit and loss account, it is a deduction from the amount due given to customers who pay their accounts within the time allowed.

Discounts received: a sundry income in the profit and loss account, it is a deduction from the amount due given to a business by a supplier when its account is paid before the time allowed has elapsed.

Dissolution: when a partnership business ceases operations and its assets are disposed of.

Double entry bookkeeping (or **double entry**): a system where each transaction is entered twice: once on the debit side of one account and once on the credit side of another account.

Drawings: funds or goods taken out (withdrawn) of a business by the owners for their private use.

Economic life of an asset (or **useful life**): the number of years before an asset wears out or becomes obsolete, whichever comes first.

Equity: another name for the owners' equity or owners' interests.

Error of omission: where a transaction is completely omitted from the books.

Error of original entry: where an item is entered, but both the debit and credit entries are of the same incorrect amount.

Error of principle: where an item is entered in the wrong type of account, e.g. a fixed asset in an expense account.

Expenses: money expended or costs incurred in a business's efforts to generate revenue (income), representing costs of doing business.

FIFO: a stock valuation method by which the earlier items held are said to be the first to be sold (first in first out).

Final accounts (or **accounts**, or **financial statements**): a term previously used to refer to financial statements produced at the end of an accounting period, such as the profit and loss account (or income statement), the balance sheet and the cashflow statement. Nowadays, the term 'financial statements' is more commonly used.

Financial statements (or **final accounts**, or **accounts**): the more common term used to refer to statements produced at the end of an accounting period to quantitatively describe the financial performance and financial position of a business, such as the profit and loss account (or income statement), the balance sheet and the cashflow statement.

Fixed assets: assets that have a long life bought with the intention to use them in the business and produce a benefit in the future and not with the intention to simply resell them.

Fixed capital accounts: capital accounts that consist only of the amounts of capital actually paid into the partnership.

Float: a small amount of money kept at hand to meet small expanses. This is also the amount at which the cash account starts each period.

General ledger (or **nominal ledger**): a ledger (central repository) for all T-accounts other than those for customers and suppliers.

Goodwill (or **purchased goodwill**): an amount representing the added value to a business of such factors as customer loyalty, reputation, intellectual property, market penetration and expertise. It is an intangible but saleable asset, and its value is not recognised in the financial statements but is realised when the business is sold.

Gross loss: where the cost of goods sold exceeds the sales revenue.

Gross profit: where the sales revenue exceeds the cost of goods sold.

Income (or **revenue**): the financial value of goods and services sold to customers.

Income statement (or **profit and loss account**): the financial statement in which the calculations of gross profit (loss) and then net profit (loss) are presented, by using the equation (profit (or loss) = revenue – expenses).

Intangible asset: an asset, such as goodwill, that has no physical existence.

Interest on capital: an amount at an agreed rate of interest that is credited to a partner's current account based on the amount of capital contributed by him/her.

Interest on drawings: an amount at an agreed rate of interest, based on the drawings taken out by a partner, which is debited to the partner's current account.

Journal: a book of original entry for all items not contained in the other books of original entry.

Liabilities: economic obligations payable to outsiders, or the debts of business arising out of past or current transactions or actions.

LIFO: a stock valuation method by which the latest items held are said to be the first to be sold (last in first out).

Limited partner: a partner whose personal liability for the business's debts is limited to the capital he/she has put into the business.

Long-term liabilities: liabilities that do not have to be paid within 12 months of the balance sheet date.

Loss: the result of selling goods for less than they cost, or the excess of expenditure over revenue.

Mark-up (cost): gross profit shown as a percentage of cost price.

Negative goodwill: the name given to the amount by which the total purchase price for a business taken over is less than the valuation of the acquired assets at that time. The amount is entered at the top of the fixed assets in the balance sheet as a negative amount.

Net assets: total assets minus total liabilities. It is an alternative term for owners' equity (or owners' interest).

Net book value: the value of a fixed asset as shown in the balance sheet. It is calculated by deducting accumulated depreciation (or provision for depreciation) from the historical cost of a fixed asset.

Net current assets (or **working capital**): current assets minus current liabilities. The figure represents the amount of resources the business has in a form that is readily convertible into cash.

Net loss: where the cost of goods sold and expenses exceeds total revenue in an accounting period.

Net profit: where sales revenue plus other revenue (income), such as rent received, exceeds the sum of cost of goods sold and other expenses.

Nominal ledger (or **general ledger**): a ledger (central repository) for all T-accounts other than those for customers and suppliers.

Overdraft: an agreed facility (or loan arrangement) granted by a bank that allows a customer holding a bank account with the bank to spend more than the funds in the account allow. Interest is normally charged daily on the amount of the overdraft on that date and the overdraft is repayable at any time upon request from the bank.

Owners' equity (or **owners' interest**, or **net assets**): capital invested by the owners, plus any new capital invested by them, minus any withdrawals made by them for personal use, plus (minus) any net profits (net losses) the business has made during the accounting period.

Owners' interest (or **owners' equity**, or **net assets**): capital invested by the owners, plus any new capital invested by them, minus any withdrawals made by them for personal use, plus (minus) any net profits (net losses) the business has made during the accounting period.

Partnership: a business in which two or more people are working together as owners, pooling money, skills and other resources with a view to making profits.

Partnership salaries: agreed amounts payable to partners in respect of duties undertaken by them. They are credited in the partner's current account.

Percentage (or **profit margin**): profit shown as percentage of the selling price.

Prepaid expense (or **prepayment**): an expense that has been paid in advance and before it is actually incurred, the benefits from which will be received in the next period. It is deducted from the relevant expense account in the profit and loss account and included in the balance sheet under current assets as 'prepayments' or 'prepaid expense'.

Prepayment (or **prepaid expense**): an expense that has been paid in advance and before it is actually incurred, the benefits from which will be received in the next period. It is deducted from the relevant expense account in the profit and loss account and included in the balance sheet as 'prepayments' or 'prepaid expense'.

Profit: the result of selling goods or services for more than they cost.

Profit and loss account (or **income statement**): the financial statement in which the calculations of gross profit (loss) and then net profit (loss) are presented, by using the equation (profit (or loss) = revenue – expenses).

Profit margin (or percentage): gross profit shown as a percentage of the selling price.

Provision for depreciation account (or **accumulated depreciation**): the account where depreciation of fixed assets is accumulated for balance sheet purposes. The accumulated depreciation is subtracted from the original cost or valuation of the asset to arrive at its net book value in the balance. The accumulated depreciation amount represents only the expired value of an asset; it is neither cash nor any other type of asset that can be used to purchase another asset.

Provision for doubtful debts (or **allowance for doubtful debts**): an account representing an estimate of the expected amount of trade debtors (i.e. debts to business) at the balance sheet date which may not paid (i.e. be irrecoverable).

Purchased goodwill (or **goodwill**): an amount representing the added value to a business of such factors as customer loyalty, reputation, intellectual property, market penetration and expertise. It is an intangible but saleable asset, and its value is not recognised in the financial statements but is realised when the business is sold.

Purchases: goods bought by the business for the prime purpose of selling them again.

Purchases returns (or **returns outwards**): goods purchased from the suppliers and subsequently returned to suppliers. Returns are deducted from the purchases figure in the profit and loss account, and are debited to the individual trade creditor's T-account.

Reducing balance method: a method of calculating depreciation in which the net book value of a fixed asset in the balance sheet is reduced every accounting year by a fixed percentage rate.

Residual value (or **scrap value**): the net amount predicted to be received from sale or disposal of a fixed asset at the end of its economic or useful life.

Returns inwards (or **sales returns**): goods already sold by the business are returned by customers sometime later. Returns are deducted from the sales figure to derive the net sales for the period, and are credited to the individual trade debtor's T-account.

Returns outwards (or **purchases returns**): goods purchased from the suppliers and subsequently returned to suppliers. Returns are deducted from the purchases figure in the profit and loss account, and are debited to the individual trade creditor's T-account.

Revaluation account: an account used to record gains and losses when assets are revalued.

Revenue (or **income**): the financial value of goods and services sold to customers.

Revenue expenditure: money expended in sales revenue, or in maintaining the business's earning capacity, including maintenance and repair of fixed assets and any other expenditures that provide a benefit lasting one year or less and are needed for the day-to-day running of the business.

Sales: cash or claims to a customer's cash from selling goods or services in the normal operations of a business.

Sales ledger: a subsidiary ledger for customers' personal accounts.

Sales returns (or **returns inwards**): goods already sold by the business are returned by customers sometime later. Returns are deducted from the sales figure to derive the net sales for the period, and are credited to the individual trade debtor's T-account.

Scrap value (or **residual value**): the net amount predicted to be received from the sale or disposal of a fixed asset at the end of its economic or useful life.

Stock (or **inventory**): goods which the business normally holds with the intention of resale. They may be finished goods, partly finished goods or raw materials awaiting conversion into finished goods that will then be sold.

Straight-line method: a method of calculating depreciation that involves deducting the same amount every accounting period from the historical cost of a fixed asset.

Suspense account: a temporary account (not included in the financial statements) in which you can enter the amount equal to the difference in the trial balance while you try to find the cause of the error(s) that resulted in the failure of the trial balance to balance.

T-account: the layout of accounts in the accounting books where the double entry bookkeeping is entered.

Trade creditor (or **trade payable**, or **account payable**): a business or person to whom money is owed for goods purchased or services rendered, or, differently, a liability owed to suppliers for goods purchases or services rendered.

Trade debtor (or **accounts receivable**): a business or person who owes money to another business for goods or services supplied, or, differently, amounts owed to a business (after selling on credit) whether or not they are currently due.

Trade discount: a deduction in price given to a trade customer (reseller) when calculating the price to be charged to that customer for some goods. It does not appear anywhere in the accounting books and so does not appear anywhere in the financial statements.

Trade payable (or **account payable**, or **trade creditor**): a business or person to whom money is owed for goods purchased or services rendered, or, differently, a liability owed to suppliers for goods purchases or services rendered.

Trial balance: a list of T-accounts and their balances in the ledgers, on a specific date, shown in debit and credit columns.

Useful life of an asset (or **economic life**): the number of years before an asset wears out or becomes obsolete, whichever comes first.

Working capital (or **net current assets**): current assets minus current liabilities. The figure represents the amount of resources the business has in a form that is readily convertible into cash.

Index

Entries in bold appear in the glossary.